FOOTBALL CHAMPIONS 2023

COLORING BOOK

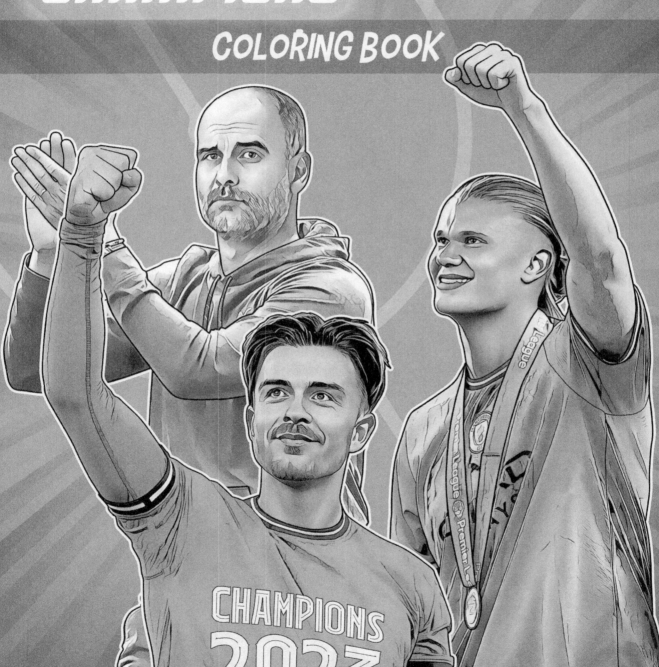

2

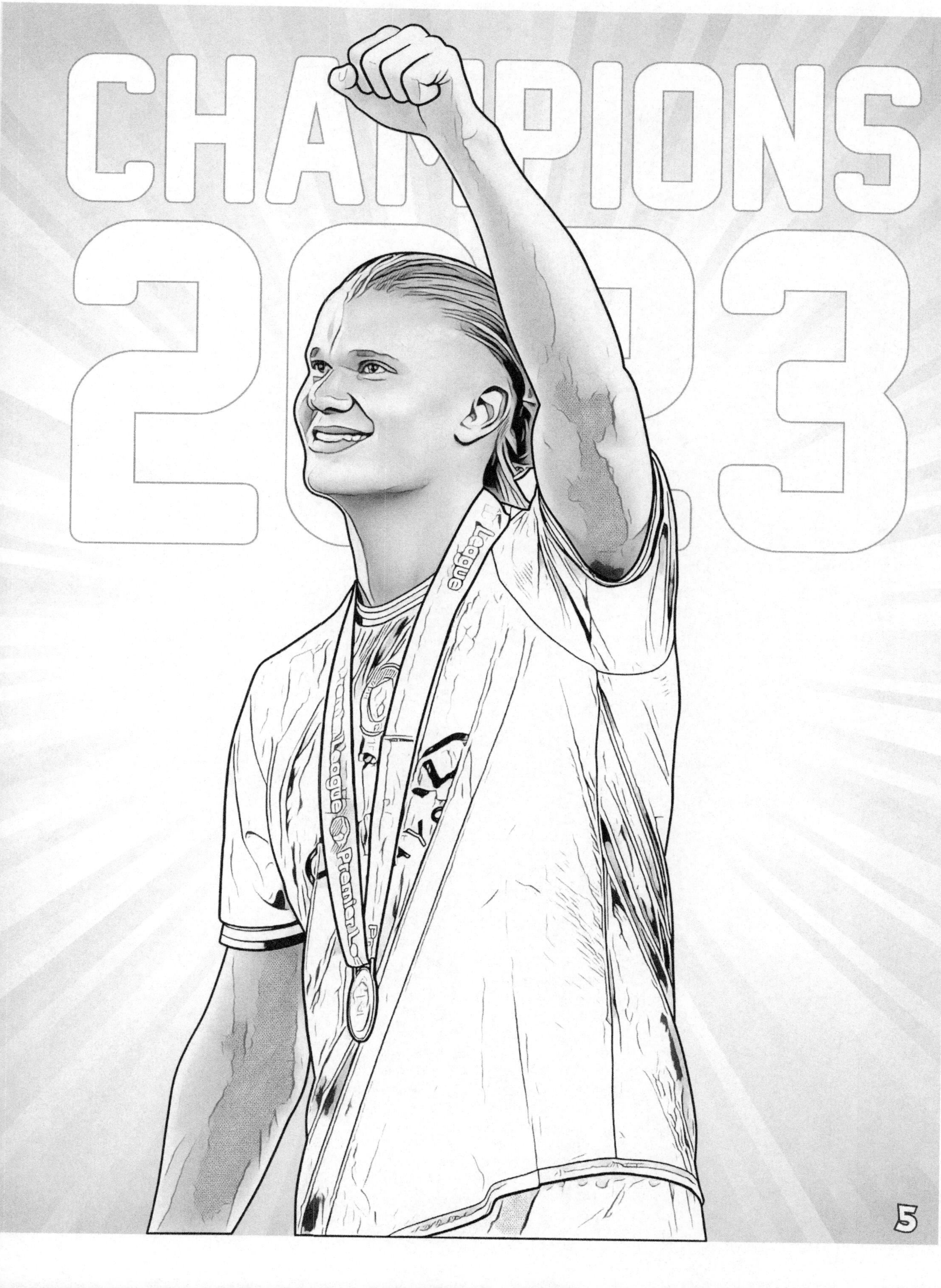
CHAMPIONS
2023

6

EDERSON

AKANJI

9

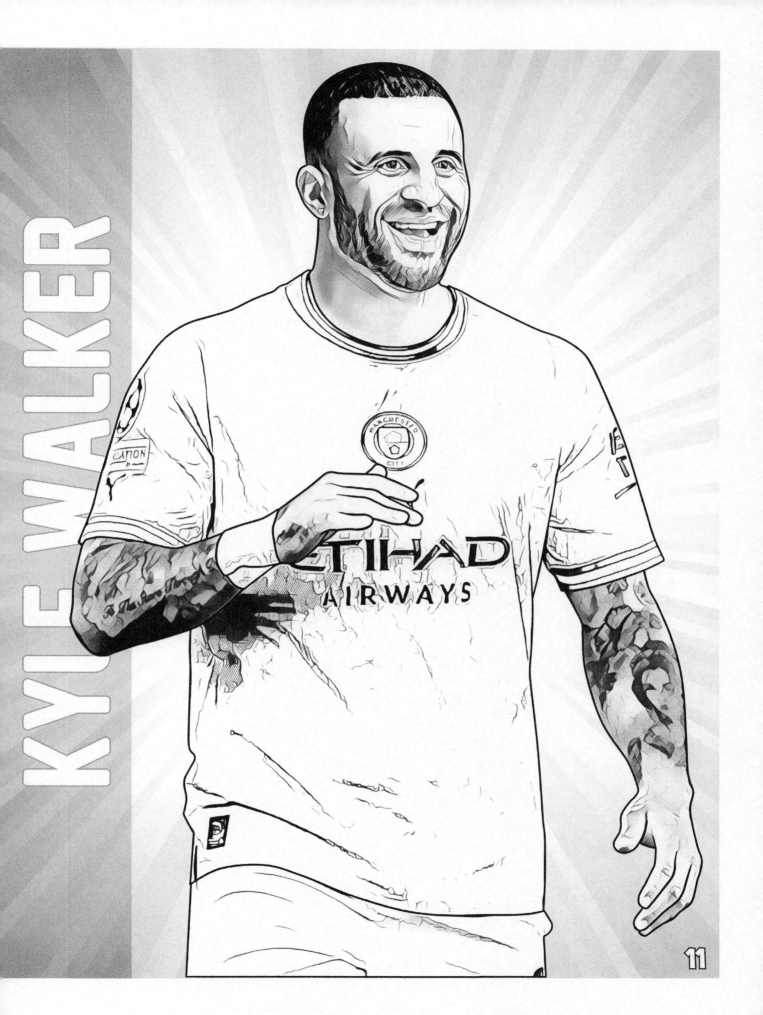

KYLE WALKER

11

AKE

13

AMERIC LAPORTE

15

JOHN STONES

17

KALVIN PHILLIPS

19

FODEN

23

BERNARDO SILVA

25

GUNDOGAN

29

KEVIN DE BRUYNE

COLE PALMER

JULIAN ALVAREZ

35

HAALAND

37

GUARDIOLA

41

JERSEY
SEASON 22.23

47

50

53

DESIGN YOUR OWN
COMMEMORATIVE JERSEYS

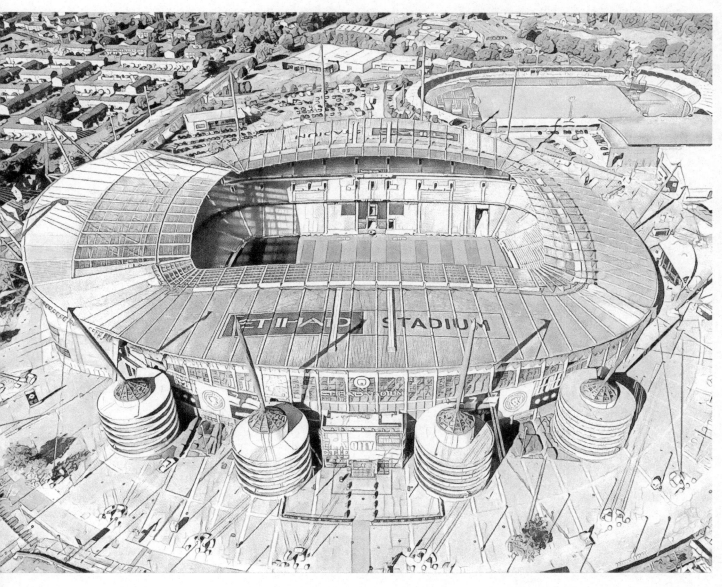

61

65

73

77

I hope you enjoyed the book.
If you liked it, leave us a nice review on
Amazon and your comments so we can keep
improving!

We really appreciate your suggestions
and we will be happy to implement your
recommendations.

Printed in Great Britain
by Amazon

35226894R00046

Spinning 101

Spinning 101

Step by Step from Fleece to Yarn with Wheel or Spindle

Tom Knisely

STACKPOLE BOOKS

Guilford, Connecticut

STACKPOLE BOOKS

An imprint of Globe Pequot, the trade division of The Rowman & Littlefield Publishing Group, Inc.
4501 Forbes Blvd., Ste. 200
Lanham, MD 20706
www.rowman.com

Distributed by NATIONAL BOOK NETWORK
800-462-6420

British Library Cataloguing in Publication Information available

Library of Congress Cataloging-in-Publication Data

Names: Knisely, Tom, author.
Title: Spinning 101: step by step from fleece to yarn with wheel or spindle / Tom Knisely.
Description: Guilford, Connecticut : Stackpole, [2021] | Summary: "In this book, Tom Knisely will teach you everything you need to know to turn raw wool into your first hand-spun yarn. He shares all of his knowledge in his easy-to-understand manner, illustrated with photographs to guide you through each of the steps"— Provided by publisher.
Identifiers: LCCN 2021013633 (print) | LCCN 2021013634 (ebook) | ISBN 9780811739153 (paperback) | ISBN 9780811769075 (epub)
Subjects: LCSH: Hand spinning. | Spun yarns.
Classification: LCC TT847 .K59 2021 (print) | LCC TT847 (ebook) | DDC 746.1/2—dc23
LC record available at https://lccn.loc.gov/2021013633
LC ebook record available at https://lccn.loc.gov/2021013634

♾™ The paper used in this publication meets the minimum requirements of American National Standard for Information Sciences—Permanence of Paper for Printed Library Materials, ANSI/NISO Z39.48-1992.

First Edition

To Ben and Reba Alexander, who owned the antique shop where I bought my first spinning wheel in 1972. They suggested that I visit another business that could help me with books on spinning and materials to spin. It was called the Mannings Handweaving School. Never did I expect that that visit would lead to my life's work.

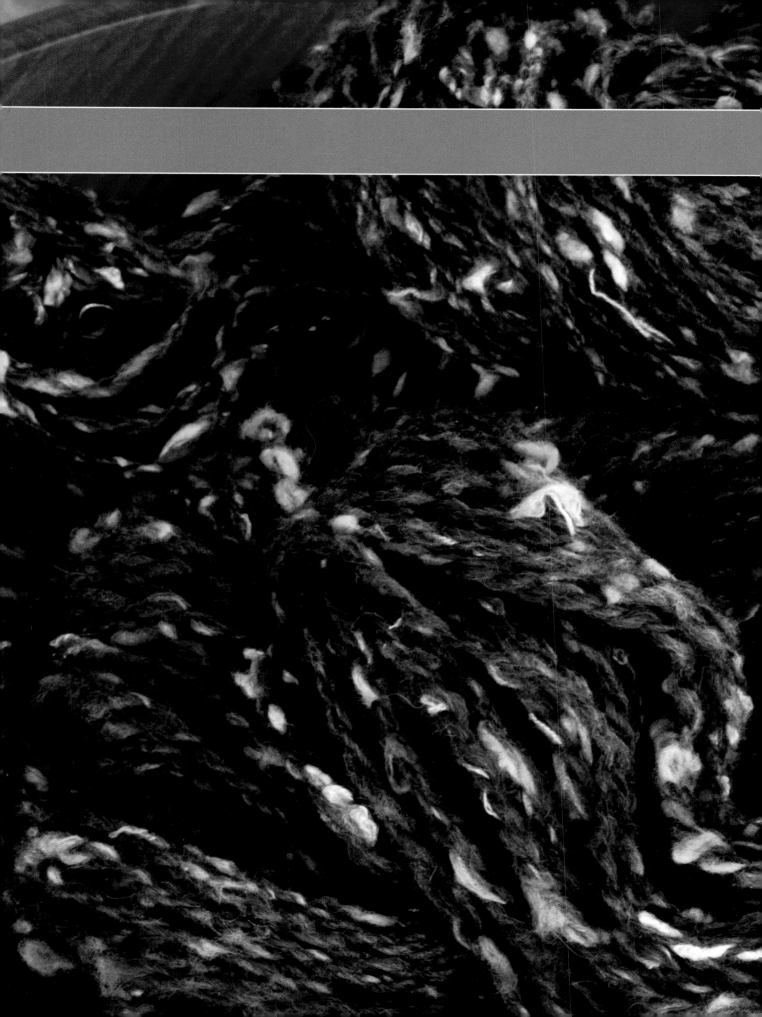

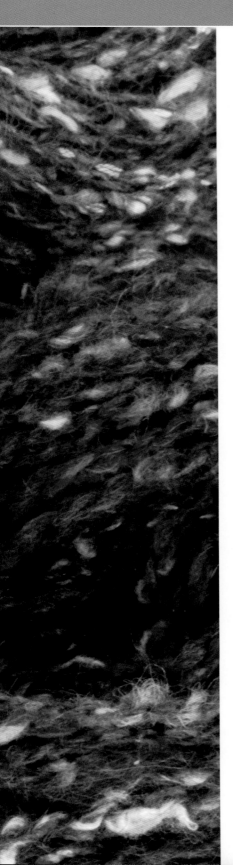

CONTENTS

Knit and Purl

So you think you want to spin your own yarns? I just have to ask you, why? I am always intrigued by the answers I get from my students when I ask them that question. The answers are fascinating and all over the spectrum. You know you are going to be asked the same question by your family and friends. "Why would you want to spin yarn?" they'll ask. "I'm sure you can buy it a whole lot cheaper than making your own." These well-meaning folks clearly don't understand the draw or passion you're experiencing in connection with the idea of taking a sheep's fleece and spinning it into yarn and then knitting or weaving it into something useful and beautiful. I get your nagging desire to spin, and I am only too happy to help you along the way with your spinning journey. Let me start by telling you my story and how I came to spin and weave, and how that led up to a forty-plus-year career of teaching others how to do the same.

As a child, I was taught by my parents to have an interest in history and antiques. When I was fourteen years old, I bought an antique spinning wheel and immediately became interested in the working mechanics of the wheel and how it twisted fibers into yarn. I bought some fleece and other fibers, as well as a book titled *Your Handspinning*, by Elsie Davenport. This was the 1970s, and there weren't self-help sites like YouTube on the Internet to go to. There wasn't even the Internet, for that matter. So I read and practiced until I was able to make a yarn on that old antique wheel. I was totally hooked! I spun and spun, making yards of yarn without a clue as to what I was going to do with it. It didn't matter, because I was having the time of my life spinning yarn and challenging myself to make yarns of different sizes and weights and also to spin different types of fibers. I looked for flax and cotton fibers to spin, and that satisfied my desire to spin the threads of early America. When I sat and spun on that old wheel, I felt a connection to history like I had never experienced in a classroom lecture. I find it hard to put words on this page to accurately describe what those moments meant to me. I was spinning yarn on a wheel that someone else had spun on before me—someone who spun to make yarn for their clothing and household textiles two hundred years ago. I was awestruck, to say the least.

Spinning could mean something totally different to another individual. For some, the idea of creating a work of art, starting from the raw material and working through the whole spinning process, and then knitting a "one of a kind" garment, would be over the top in their mind. This scenario reminds me of my friend Fran. She and her husband sold their home in suburbia and moved to a farm in the country. Fran now had the farm and needed a couple of sheep. Along came two Romney ewes. One was named Knit; the other was named Purl. In the spring, when the girls were shorn, Fran dyed their fleece and spun the wool into a bulky weight yarn to knit into a sweater. One day I ran into Fran and asked, "How is it going down on the farm?" Fran gave me a big hug and told me she was living her dream. She realized it when she went to the barn one frosty fall morning to feed Knit and Purl. Before leaving the house, Fran slipped on the sweater she had spun and knitted from her beautiful sheep.

When she was finished doing her barn chores, she thanked Knit and Purl for their contribution to her lovely warm sweater. Fran loved not only her sweater but also the symbiotic relationship she had with her sheep. She said, "It's hard to explain to someone. How many people can say they know the source of their sweater's yarn? You don't get that from a store rack." I totally understood what Fran was saying, and it made my heart happy to know she got it as well.

Whatever your reason for wanting to spin, I can tell you right now that you are going to enjoy it. Spinning is a skill that takes patience and practice at first, but once you got it, well, you got it. Welcome aboard as we travel through these chapters together and I help you get to your spinning dreams and destinations.

Happy spinning,
Tom Knisely

1

Of Fleece and Fibers

I have always started my beginning spinners off with spinning wool. As your teacher, I think it's important to set you up for success. Wool in general is an easy fiber to prepare and spin. I know there will be people who tell me that they don't like wool next to their skin because it's scratchy to the touch. Yes, I know this may be true, but please bear with me—there are many different degrees of scratchy. I see wool as a little like people: some are soft and pleasant to be around, and others are, well, scratchy and irritate you down to your very last nerve. So, for now, let's avoid working with the scratchy, coarse wools and get you familiar with the pleasant varieties. Once you have become comfortable with your basic spinning skills, I am going to encourage you to try other spinning fibers such as mohair, alpaca, llama, and even silk. We also don't want to forget the plant fibers, known as cellulose fibers. These include cotton, hemp, and flax (linen). Your spinning world is about to explode with all the possibilities before you. But let's slow down just a little and concentrate on the basics, starting with how to choose a good fleece.

I would suggest that you become familiar with the different breeds of sheep and what a particular breed's fleece is recognized for. There are breeds such as Merino and Ramboulet that have very fine wool and have set the standards for softness in fleece. On the other side of the spectrum, there are breeds raised for hard-wearing wool yarns that might be used for carpeting or other tough fabrics. These fleeces are more like coarse, straight hair and would definitely be uncomfortable to wear close to your skin. Karakul is a breed that comes to mind in this category, and these fleeces are generally spun for carpeting.

When fleeces are graded by a professional wool grader, they are given a numerical grade according to their fineness, which follows a recognized standard in the wool trade. The grades go from 1 to 100. The lower the number, the coarser the wool, and the higher the number, the finer the wool. It's fascinating to watch a grader at work. Their sensitive, trained hands and fingers can quickly identify the correct category for a fleece, which helps buyers know the quality of the wool they are about to purchase. This information is most important for a wool yarn manufacturer, who has to maintain a consistent quality to the yarn from year to year. For the average spinner such as you and me, I think it is enough to know whether we are going to be buying coarse, medium, or fine wools.

So at this point I know you are asking yourself, "Where do I buy a fleece? What kind should I buy?" I want to start by telling you that you are the luckiest spinner I know. You have all kinds of options available to you. There is the Internet. Shepherds now have websites and use the Internet to sell their fleeces. When you reach out and contact these farms, they often offer to send samples for you to see and touch.

I like to see and feel the wool I'm about to buy, so I try to attend local fiber festivals in my area. I live on the East Coast, so every May it's off to the Maryland Sheep and Wool Festival. The fall brings the New York State Wool Festival. WARNING! It's easy to get caught up in the excitement of the day and come home with a car full of fleece. There are plenty of experts at these festivals who will help you choose a fleece. Before you go, it's probably a good thing to become familiar with some of the various breeds of sheep and the type of wool they grow. I have included here in the book some photos of locks of wool from several breeds of sheep to help you with your choices. There is, of course, nothing better than just leaping in and purchasing samples of fleece and spinning it up to make your own

Border Leicester sheep have a large stocky frame and often have a fleece weight of 10 pounds or more. Fleeces can have a staple length of 6–8 inches. They are lustrous in appearance and spin into a lovely sweater yarn.

Cormo sheep share bloodlines of both Merino and Corriedale sheep. This breed produces a fleece with a staple length of 4–6 inches and a fleece weight of 9–12 pounds. Cormo is a joy to spin, and the finished yarn is soft enough for wearing apparel.

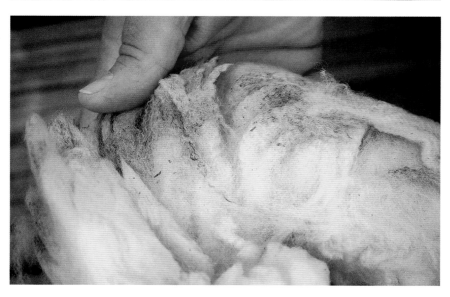

The Corriedale breed is a result of crossing Lincoln or English Leicester rams with Merino ewes. The result is a breed with a finer fleece and a longer staple length. It has a well-defined crimp to the staple. The fleece is 10–13 pounds and has a typical staple length of 3–5 inches.

The Corriedale Cormo Cross fleece has all the wonderful qualities of both breeds. It spins into a very useful knitting and weaving yarn. Although cross-breed sheep don't always give you a true example of what the standard wool is from each parent, these fleeces can be beautiful and a pleasure to spin. Don't discount a cross-breed fleece. I would much rather spin a clean cross-breed fleece than a dirty pure-breed.

Dorsets are medium-size sheep that are better known for their lean meat. The Dorset fleece is rather short, with a staple length of 2–4 inches. It has a springy crimp and is often blended with other fleeces to add elasticity to the spun yarn. This fleece spins into a wonderful knitting yarn.

The Florida Cracker is one of the oldest breeds in North America. It is believed to have been brought by the Spanish in the sixteenth century. The wool has a short staple and lacks lanolin. It is a medium-grade wool that is suitable for woven blankets and knitwear.

Romneys are medium-size sheep, and the wool has a well-defined crimp to the staple. The wool has luster and spins into a lovely knitting yarn suitable for sweaters and outer garments. Fleece weighs 8–12 pounds and has a 5- to 8-inch staple length.

comparisons and see for yourself what wools you like and what you don't like. I suggest you go to a wool festival and try to talk to the shepherds themselves and ask them why they have chosen the breed they raise. The answers are often fascinating. Then see whether you can buy a small amount of different wools to spin and compare. Keep good notes. Then put your fleece samples, spun samples, and notes in a binder, and you will have an invaluable resource to return to again and again.

Now, if any of you are thinking that buying a fleece and preparing it for spinning is not for you, don't despair. You don't need to go through all that prep work. There are many wool merchants who sell wool ready to spin. Some even offer breed-specific prepared fiber for spinners. These wools are usually sold as roving, combed top, or sliver. Roving is wool that has been washed and carded commercially. It looks like a fluffy rope. Wool spun from roving is considered woolen spun yarn. Combed top and sliver are more refined and spin into a smooth and lustrous thread.

Now let me give you a few pointers on what to look for when buying your first fleece. I look for the overall cleanliness of the fleece. If at first glance it is covered with lots of hay, grass, and other vegetal matter, you want to avoid it. A small amount of hay is not unusual. After all, sheep sleep in their bedding of straw and graze for food in a pasture; they are sure to pick up some unwanted vegetal matter in their fleece. This is known as "VM" in spinning circles. However, you could spend hours trying to pick and shake out all those tiny bits so they don't become part of your spun yarn.

After a shearer has finished clipping the wool from the sheep, it's not unusual for them to take some

time to perform other necessary services the sheep may require. This is especially true with a small flock of sheep that are to be shorn and where time is not the most important part of the shearing process. The shearer can take a little more time with each sheep and do a better job. After the fleece has been shorn from the sheep, a second person usually pulls the fleece away from the sheering area and rolls it up into a neat bundle, ties it with a cord, and places it in a plastic bag for storage. The shearer then trims hooves and gives shots and releases the sheep back into the pasture. The canvas tarp that was used for the staging area is then swept clean before the next sheep is to be shorn. If this systematic routine is maintained, the fleeces stay relatively clean. However, if this routine is not kept up and the staging area is allowed to get dirty, you can get all sorts of undesirable inclusions added to the rolled bundle of fleece.

When buying a fleece, be sure to ask whether it has been skirted. A skirted fleece is one that has been unrolled and gone through to remove the dirty and unwanted areas of the shorn fleece (see Figure 1). This might include the neck, legs, belly wool, and the wool toward the rear of the sheep that is dirty from dung and urine staining. When I am buying a skirted fleece, I expect to be buying only the fleece that covered the back and sides and from the shoulders to the rump. I also look for something called "second cuts" (see Figure 2). Second cuts are the short pieces of wool that are made when the shearer passes their clippers over an area on the sheep that has already been shorn. I come to the defense of shearers everywhere when I say that second cuts are not always the result of poor shearing or inexperience. Sometimes a sheep will

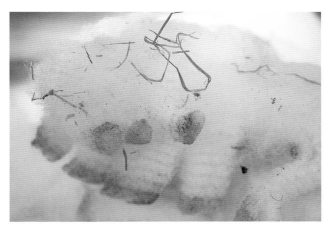

Figure 1. Look for a skirted fleece that does not include stains and excessive vegetal matter.

Figure 2. Second cuts are short pieces of wool that are made when the shearer passes their clippers over an area on a sheep that has already been shorn. Too many of these are undesirable.

Figure 3. Sometimes a dark fleece may have sun-bleached tips. This is OK; these tips can be either cut or blended into your yarn for a heathery effect.

move and wiggle while being shorn, and the shearer can't help but re-clip an area and get short lengths of wool. These second cuts are undesirable and result in bumps or slubs in the yarn. You need to be sure to look for an excess of second cuts in the fleece, and a well-skirted fleece will have very few of them.

Also look out for what is called a "sick fleece." This is a weak spot in the lock of wool as a result of the animal being sick. Take a lock of the fleece (also known as a staple), hold it tightly between the tip end and shorn end, and give it a sharp tug; if it breaks in the middle, you are looking at a sick fleece. You want to avoid a fleece such as this because the locks will break up into short lengths during the washing and processing before spinning the wool into yarn.

Weakened or brittle tip ends are not unusual and are not to be confused with a sick fleece. Brittle tip ends are the result of the fleece being exposed and weathered by rain and snow and wear. These ends can be removed easily while picking the fleece before carding it. Dark-colored fleeces will sometimes show sun bleaching at the tips (see Figure 3). These lighter-colored tips can be either cut away or blended into the wool when carding to create a heathery look to the yarn. Some shepherds will cover their sheep with fabric coats to prevent sun bleaching and the weathering process. The coats are placed on the sheep immediately after shearing when the sheep body is the cleanest. Throughout the year, as the fleece grows in length, the shepherd will replace the coats with larger ones to accommodate the sheep's expanding girth. A single sheep may wear several coats between shearings. These protected fleeces are beautiful, and the pricing of a coated fleece is reflected at the sales table.

It is my recommendation that you purchase the best-quality fleece that you can find and also afford. A dirty fleece that has a lot of vegetal matter may be inexpensive but is not one worth spending a great deal of time on. As the saying goes, "You get what you pay for."

Washing Your Fleece

If this is your first time washing sheep wool (also known as scouring), your thoughts might go from totally overwhelmed at the daunting task to a "that's a piece of cake" attitude. I'll tell you right now, the reality is somewhere in between. You do need to be careful in your handling of the wool and with fluctuation in water temperature. You can't just throw the fleece into your washing machine and walk away like you might with a load of gardening clothes. If you do, the results could look like a hairy dumpling weighing several pounds. You want to avoid felting your fleece, and so a couple of simple and easy rules need to be remembered and followed. I'll get to all of that in just a moment, but first I want to tell you two stories about why you might want to wash your fleece.

I started spinning in the 1970s. It was in the height of the "back to the land" movement, and folks were driven to live and lead a more natural way of life. Since the oils that sheep secrete (lanolin) are natural, well, it just seemed right to spin yarn in what is known as spinning "in the grease." This means taking the fleece after it's been shorn from the sheep and spinning your wool yarn without washing it. YUK! I say this to you now, but spinning in the grease was the mindset at the time. I didn't take into consideration what else might be in that fleece—namely, dung, urine, and dirt. I unknowingly spun pounds and pounds of yarn with dust and dirt trapped within the twist of the yarn, all for the sake of not losing all that lovely lanolin. I also remember my spinning wheel, carders, and other equipment being covered with grease and dirt. It was only after the wool was spun and plied and made into skeins that I washed the skeins. Now, in spite of the fact that people have been washing fleece and spinning yarn for hundreds of years, I was going to go against convention and spin my yarn in an artsy, hippie-like manner. I was going to spin in the grease like the other spinners I hung out with.

One day I had volunteered to spin at a local crafters event. I spun my dirty, unwashed wool all morning. When lunchtime came, I ignored my filthy hands and ate my sandwich along with a few oatmeal and carob cookies and an apple. Later that day I became quite ill—so sick that I will never forget the feeling. It wasn't until much later that I realized that along with the yummy lunch fare, I had consumed dirt, dung, and grease from my unwashed hands. That was a lesson well learned and never forgotten. I then decided to wash my fleeces from that day onward.

My second story involves a carding machine that was used to straighten and prepare wool for spinning. A customer came into the shop where I worked with a carding machine that needed to have the carding cloth replaced. The teeth were rusted and brittle. As you turned the carding drum, the teeth broke off when they lightly touched one another. The wood and other parts of the carder were embedded with dirt and grime. When I asked the customer what had happened to this carder, they told me that it had been stored in an attic with a carded batt of unwashed wool left on the drum. It had been in the attic for several years that way. Perhaps the dirt and urine in the wool caused the metal teeth to corrode and become weak and brittle. The manufacturer replaced the carding cloth and cleaned the carder. That was the first and last time I ever saw anything like it.

Carding mills and woolen mills wash fleeces before they put them through their equipment. It is not a difficult task. Here are a few simple rules to follow at home.

1. Sort and pick out any dung and manure tags that you see in the fleece. Also remove hay, straw, grass, or other vegetal matter that's clinging to the fleece.

2. Work with small amounts by weight. A pound of raw fleece is easy to wash and dry and takes some time to spin up. I do it in shifts. Wash, dry, and spin. While I am spinning the first batch, the second and third batches can be washing and drying. You don't have to do it all at once.

3. I wash my fleece in several wash tubs: one for washing and several for rinsing. You want them large enough to hold several gallons of hot water. A canner with a lid can help you keep your water temperatures hot for a longer period of time.

4. Yes, that's correct, HOT WATER! I know this goes against everything your parents told you about washing wool. We have all heard the stories of the shrunken sweater. Hot water alone is not the enemy. Hot water, cold rinse, and the agitation of a washing machine were your sweater's worst nightmare. Lanolin and suint (sheep sweat) start to melt away at 120 degrees or greater. These temperatures are not too hot. You need these higher temperatures to properly clean wool, especially fleeces with a naturally higher lanolin content such as Merino and other fine-wool sheep. When dyeing yarns, I often have my

First, pick through your fleece and pull out any second cuts or vegetal matter.

You will need several large pots of hot water.

Use hot water and Dawn dish detergent to soak and wash your wool. Handle with heat-resistant gloves or tongs to avoid burns.

Spread your fleece out on a sweater rack to dry.

dye pots at a low simmer, and that's hot. It doesn't harm my skeins and won't harm your wool to be exposed to those higher temperatures. Use gloves when handling this hot wool and transferring it from the wash water to the rinse tubs. A lingerie bag can be a help with washing your fleece. It contains the fleece and makes it easy to transfer from wash tub to rinse tub. I use Dawn dish detergent to wash my fleece at about ¼ cup of Dawn to a pound or two of fleece and depending on the amount of lanolin, wool waxes, and suint there is in the fleece. Be sure to use a lot of hot water. The higher the ratio of hot water to wool, the better. Fifteen to twenty minutes in the wash water is all you need. Carefully lift the wool out of the wash water and gently squeeze out the soapy water. Place the fleece in the hot rinse water and let it soak there for ten minutes. Remove again and transfer into another tub of hot rinse water. It's important to keep the water temperatures similar. Do not shock the fleece.

5. When the water appears to be clear in the last rinse, remove the fleece and squeeze it with your hands to remove most of the water. You can put it into a washing machine set for SPIN ONLY. The centrifugal force that removes water from your clothes will also remove the excess water from your fleece without doing harm. If you use a lingerie bag to wash your fleece, you can also go outside and swing it over your head for several minutes—it will do the same job. Think about all the material you will provide your neighbors for talking about you.

6. Drying your newly cleaned wool is rather easy. I like using sweater racks or using a frame with wire or nylon screening stretched to the frame. Having air circulation around the fleece helps in the drying process. Put your fleece outside on a sunny, beautiful day. It will be dry in a few hours. On a cold day in the winter months when I have decided to wash fleece, I might dry it indoors on sweater racks set over a few bath towels located on a spare bed; you can also put a drying rack on a table or the floor—anywhere there's good circulation of air. Toss it several times throughout the drying process to get that air moving all around the fleece.

7. Thoroughly dried fleeces can be stored in airtight containers away from mice and moths. I have found a few dryer sheets placed in the container do wonders to keep unwanted beasties away. Now that your fleece is washed and cleaned, it is ready for the next step. That next step is to card or comb the wool in preparation for spinning it into yarn. Let's go to the next chapter on wool preparation.

Preparing the Wool for Spinning

Many people will tell you how they appreciate a delicious meal, but they will also admit that they don't enjoy the lengthy preparation and cooking that goes into making that meal. So, like a mid-week grab-and-go takeout dinner, many spinners will purchase prepared fiber so that they can just sit down and start spinning right away. Other spinners will tell you that they love the whole process of fiber preparation. They love the choosing of the fleece, washing it, and making the decision to card or comb the wool depending on whether they want a woolen-spun yarn or worsted-spun yarn. What's that, you ask? Let's start here by explaining the difference between woolen-spun and worsted-spun yarns (see Figure 4).

Woolen-spun yarns are recognized by their soft, lofty, gentle twist in the yarn. These wools are carded either by hand carders or through the use of a drum carder. Before carding, the spinner must first pick the wool to open up the fibers (see Figure 5). This process transforms the tight locks of wool into a fluffy cloud. As you pick your wool, you will notice small pieces of chaff and dirt dropping down onto your lap or the ground around you. Picking also gives you the opportunity to remove larger pieces of hay and grass or even the occasional short second cuts of wool. If the tip ends are brittle, pull on the tips and break them off and discard them. Second cuts and brittle tips add bumps and unevenness to your yarns as you spin. This is a task that's best done outside, but if the weather is inclement, find a place indoors that provides easy cleanup of the floor. I will sometimes lay an old sheet on the floor where I am going to sit. Find a comfortable chair to sit

Figure 4. Worsted-spun yarn (left) is prepared by combing (with the fibers all parallel) and is strong and smooth, while woolen-spun yarn (right) is prepared by carding (with fibers not all aligned) and is lofty and gently twisted.

Figure 5. Picking your wool is a process of pulling fibers apart to loosen and free them from dirt.

on, and place the washed fleece on one side of you and an empty basket or bag on the other side to hold your newly picked wool. Now, as you sit and pick your fleece, the small bits of dirt will fall down in front of you and onto the sheet, making for some easy cleanup. Picking wool by yourself can almost put you into a meditative state. It's productive work even when you want to enjoy a little personal, alone time. You could also host a picking party with a few spinner friends. After all, many hands make light work, as I have been told. Avoid serving messy, sticky finger foods to your guests at your picking party.

Now you're ready to start carding your picked wool. Or are you? Why do we card or comb the fleece before spinning? The answer is really quite simple: We developed carders and combs to align the fibers to make the spinning easier and to also spin a smooth and uniform thread. If your goal is to spin a rustic yarn with thick and thin areas along the length of the yarn, then you want to try spinning from the picked wool and reject the notion of straightening or aligning those wool fibers. Just hold a small amount of that picked wool and start spinning right from it. Now, they say beauty is in the eyes of the beholder, and a rustic-looking yarn may be just what you are seeking. There is a movement by some folks to spin avant-garde or "art yarns." These yarns are beautiful and just the right thing in some applications but not all. A cable-knit sweater knitted from art yarn is not going to define the beautiful nature of the cable. The clean, architectural structure of the cable will be lost. A sweater with cables needs to be knitted with smooth yarns. A sweater knitted with a simple design or a blanket woven with a plain weave structure will best show off these rustic yarns. Art yarn is best used with simple patterning to show off the yarn. You want to accentuate the yarns, not the pattern.

I find it fascinating to see how trends come and go and how some people might look at these art yarns as imperfections and others embrace the rustic look. For years, spinners looked to the right tools to help spin the most uniform yarns, and now we embrace the polar opposite. There is a place for all yarns.

Hand Carding

Hand carding has been used by spinners for hundreds of years to straighten wool fibers in preparation for spinning woolen-spun yarns. As mentioned before, these yarns have a soft and lofty appearance. This is due to the arrangement of the carded fibers and the way the spinner introduces twist into the yarn. The spinner uses what is known as a "long draw" to spin these yarns. We'll talk more about that in the upcoming chapter on spinning techniques. Right now, let's talk about carding and how to make a rolag.

If you watch several spinners carding or ask them how to card wool, you will most likely get a different answer from each individual. There are a couple of things you must always remember to do. The first thing to remember is to not overload the carders. Work with smaller amounts for a better job. The other thing to remember is to not push the carders' teeth too deeply into each other. The teeth should just touch, and the carding action should be light. Approach the carding like you are brushing a child's hair or brushing your pet. Brush lightly but deliberately. Start by finding a pair of carders that fit your hands comfortably. I personally like a pair of carders with a slight curve. Standard wool carders have carding cloth with seventy-two teeth per square inch. Carders with finer teeth and more teeth per square inch are better suited to card cotton and finer fibers such as cashmere. The teeth should give a little when you push against them with your fingers. You don't want them too stiff. Hand carders are sold as a pair, and they are identical. In the past, people would tell you to mark your carders with an "R" on one carder and an "L" on the other carder. I believe this was to aid and give clarity to written instructions on how to card (for instance, take the right carder to the left). What it did was add confusion to my mind. It left me with the impression that if I ever exchanged carders into the opposite hands, I would do irreversible damage to the teeth. NOT SO. The carders are identical. I like to think about the carders this way: one is the active carder, and the other is the passive carder. This will help describe the process for both right- and left-handed dominance.

OK, you're ready to go. Find a comfortable chair to sit on. I am right-handed, so I will place one carder on my left knee. While holding the handle of the carder to add stability, charge the carder with a small amount of picked wool (see Figure 6). The term "charged" means placing the wool onto the teeth of the passive carder

Figure 6. Fill, or charge, the passive carder with wool by placing wool onto the teeth and dragging the fibers away from the handle so that some are caught in the teeth.

and gently dragging the fibers away from the handle so they engage with the teeth of the carder. Fill the carding cloth, but don't over-fill it. Now, with the active carder in my right hand, I will start to gently brush, or card, the wool (see Figure 7). Do not push the active carder too deeply into the teeth of the passive carder. The goal is to have the teeth of the carders just touch one another. I visualize the passive carder's surface area as having three sections. The first is near the front of the carder, or the toe. Then there is the second or middle portion, and lastly there is the third portion (or heel) of the carder. So, like brushing a child's hair, starting at the bottom and working my way to the part in the scalp, I start to card at the toe with the first stroke of my active carder before moving to the middle and then to the third, or heel, section. I then continue with several full-length strokes of the active carder to straighten the fibers. You will notice that there will be wool attaching itself to the active carder. This is totally normal.

Now turn the active carder so that the handles are together on the same side. Lightly place the toe of the active carder near the heel of the passive carder and gently push the active carder away from you (see Figure 8). This magically transfers the fibers from the active carder back onto the passive carder on your lap. Continue carding several more times until the fibers start to look aligned on the passive carder.

You might think you are finished and ready to remove the wool, but not yet. What you can't see are the fibers on the underside of the passive carder. They have not had the benefit of being properly carded. Near the end of the carding, bring the carder handles to the same side. Now, transfer the wool on the

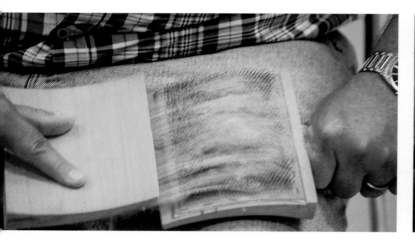

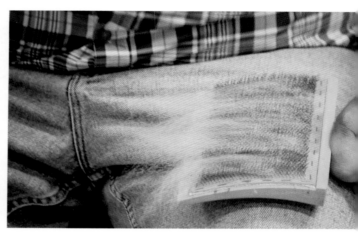

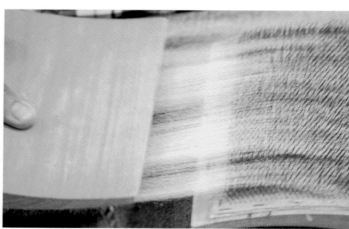

Figure 7. Start to brush with your active carder, moving from toe to middle to heel.

passive carder to the active carder the same way, by placing the toe of the passive carder near the heel of the active carder and gently transferring the wool onto the bed of the active carder (see Figure 9).

Now the wool is located on the active carder. Return to the original positions with the empty passive carder on your left leg and the active carder in your right hand with the wool attached to the bed of the carder. Card again in the same manner that you have been doing, and the underside will have a chance to get carded. After several more swipes of the active carder, it will be time to move all the carded wool to the

Figure 8. Place the toe of the active carder near the heel of the passive carder and gently push away to transfer the fibers from the active carder back onto the passive carder.

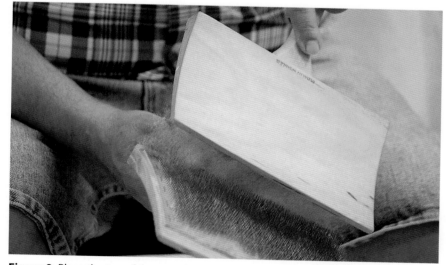

Figure 9. Place the toe of the passive carder to the heel of the active carder and gentry transfer the wool onto the bed of the active carder.

Figure 10. Hand-carded wool becomes rolags for spinning.

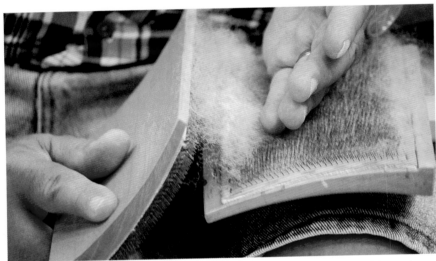

Figure 11. With the passive carder resting on your leg, use the toe end of the active carder to lift the wispy ends of the carded wool, using your hand to help get it started.

Figure 12. Make a rolag by rolling the wool in the same direction as the teeth on the passive carder are bent.

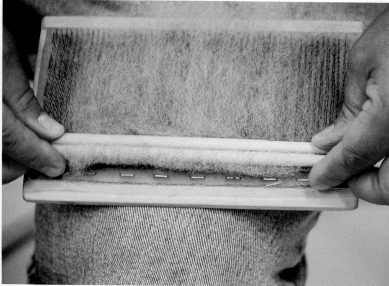
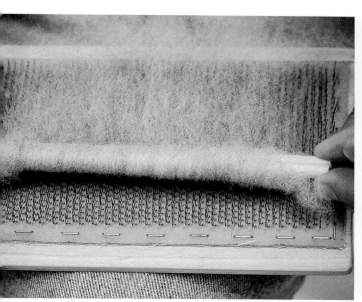

Figure 13. Two dowels may also be used to roll your fiber. Capture the ends of the wool between the dowels, roll the wool, and then slide out the dowels.

passive carder. Return the handles of the carders to the same side. Place the toe of the active carder at the heel end of the passive carder and push the active carder gently away from you. This will put the wool on the bed of the passive carder. You are now ready to remove the fiber in a form known as a rolag (see Figure 10). With the passive carder resting on your left leg, use the toe end of the active carder to lift the wispy ends of the carded wool (see Figure 11). Use the edge of your left hand to help get started. Push and roll the wool in the same direction as the teeth

on the passive carder are bent (see Figure 12). Using the active carder to help, you are now turning this carded wool into a rolag. I think of the process like making a jelly roll or a burrito. You can also use two well-sanded and smooth dowel rods to help in making a rolag (see Figure 13). Trap the overhanging wisps of wool between the dowels and hold the dowels tightly in both hands. Now roll the dowels toward the handle of the carder and remove the wool. Slide the dowels out, and you have a rolag. Since rolags spin up quickly, I will sometimes take an evening to sit and make rolags.

Carding with a Drum Carder

Having a drum carder to prepare your fleece is a great help and speeds up the carding process. It's much like the difference between a paring knife and a food processor. The most common drum carder design has two cylinders, or "drums," with carding cloth wrapped around them. You will notice that they are very different in size. The small drum near the feeding tray is known as the "licker" drum (see Figure 14). Its function is to pick up the picked wool fibers from the feeding tray and transfer them onto the "carding" drum, which is much larger in circumference (see Figure 15). There is a crank handle attached to the carding drum that, when turned clockwise, moves the carding drum clockwise. A belt or chain that is attached to the carding drum also moves the licker drum in a counterclockwise direction, and the teeth of the licker drum pick up the wool and place it against the teeth of the carding drum (see Figure 16). The distance between the drums is very close. As the two drums revolve, the fibers begin to get straightened. Many carders have drums with eight-inch-wide carding cloth. This helps to card a great deal of wool onto the carding drum. I have been able to card as much as two to three ounces of wool into what is known as a "batt." I slowly feed the wool onto the feeding tray and card until the wool builds up on the carding drum. When I see the wool has come up to the top of the teeth of the carding drum, I stop. There is no more room to accept more wool.

Stop at this point and look for an obvious gap between the teeth of the carding drum (see Figure 17). This is the space where you will tear the wool free from the carder. Using a tool called a doffer, you want

Figure 14. The small drum near the feeding tray is the licker drum.

Figure 15. The licker drum pulls the fiber from the feeding tray to the larger drum known as the carding drum.

Figure 16. Carding drums may be manual or hand cranked. As the drums turn, they pull the fibers into alignment.

to push the doffer under the carded batt and lift up to tear and separate the batt. You may need to do this in several small attempts to make it easier. When the batt is separated along the line of the carder, grab the ends of the batt and pull up (see Figure 18). The carding drum will be turning counterclockwise, and your carded batt will peel free from the carding drum (see Figure 19). This does a fine job initially, but for the best spinning batts, I run the wool through several more times to make sure that I have done a really good job of carding my fibers.

A carding machine is ideal for carding a variety of fibers. Wools of different lengths can all be carded. For instance, a long-stapled wool such as Lincoln Long Wool, with a staple length of 7–8 inches, will card beautifully on a drum carder because of the large surface area of the carding drum. Otherwise, you would have two options for this lustrous long wool: either

Figure 17. The carding drum will have an obvious gap between its teeth in one area. Insert a tool called a doffer into this groove, under the wool, and pull it up to separate.

Figure 18. When the wool is separated, grab the ends and pull up to remove your carded batt.

Figure 19. The wool batt is removed from the carder. If you want even more parallel fibers, run the same wool through the carder several more times.

comb it for a worsted-spun yarn or cut it in half to fit the carding bed of your hand carders.

A drum carder is also ideal for doing fiber blending. A wool and alpaca or wool and mohair blend is much more easily blended using a drum carder because of the large surface areas of carding cloth. The color blending of dyed fleece for spinning a heathered yarn is also much easier and more uniform. When starting out with the first initial run, I alternate the fibers or colors on the feeding tray (see Figure 20). I continue this way until I have made my batt; then I remove it from the carding machine as described before. At this point, the fibers are only roughly blended. I then tear the batt into small pieces called planks (see Figure 21). Next, I place the small planked bits of batt on the feeding tray perpendicular to the licker roller. This is how I will present the wool to the drum along with all the other pieces from the original batt. This does an amazing job of blending the fibers. After making the second batt and removing it from the carder, look at it to see whether you feel it is blended to your liking. If you feel it needs to be blended more, plank the batt and run it again for the third time. This will surely do the job.

Figure 20. Alternate colors on the feeding tray for blended colors, such as those for a heathered yarn.

Figure 21. To combine further, tear the batt into small pieces, or planks, and place them on the feeding tray perpendicular to the licker roller.

Combing

Wool combs look very different from hand carders. The teeth are long and very sharp so that they can easily pass through the long, washed staples of fiber. Combs are designed to straighten the fibers so that they lie parallel to each other. When spinning combed fiber, the spinner uses a short draw technique to control the twist as it enters the perfectly aligned fibers. The result is a strong, smooth yarn without the loftiness of a woolen-spun yarn. The technique for spinning a worsted yarn will be shown in chapter 6, which is dedicated to spinning techniques. I like using a worsted-spun yarn for rug warp or where I want the finished fabric to be strong and hard wearing. I also like the lustrous look of a worsted-spun yarn. The luster is partly due to the preparation but also due to the type of fiber being combed. Long-stapled wool and hair fibers such as mohair and suri alpaca fibers have a natural luster to them. That luster remains even after washing, combing, and using the yarn in your project.

There are several different styles of combs to be had. I stick with my two favorites: Viking combs and English combs (see Figure 22). Viking combs will have one or two rows of long, stainless steel tines. These are good combs for preparing long-stapled wool. The English combs have five rows of tines in different sizes and are mounted on an angle. English combs are good for long- and shorter-stapled fibers and are the most versatile combs, in my opinion.

Here is how to use them: Start by placing one comb in its mounting block, tines up toward the ceiling, and tighten it down so it can't move. Then carefully place and pull the washed locks of wool down onto the comb tines so that the wool is close to the base of the tines (see Figure 23). Continue to add locks until you are

Figure 22. Viking combs have one or two rows of long tines. English combs have five rows of tines in different sizes and are mounted at an angle.

about one-quarter of the way up the tines and stop there. This will be known as the stationary or passive comb. Now carefully unlock the tensioning screw while holding the comb. Turn the comb so that the tines are facing the right if you are right-handed and toward the left if you are left-handed (see Figure 24). Retighten the tensioning knob to hold the comb from moving. With the second comb in your hand, bring it down as if you are using a hammer and engage the tines of the active comb into the tip ends of the wool (see Figure 25). Let the tines of the active comb go all the way through so the tips meet with the base of the active comb, and then pull the active comb back toward you

to free it. Do this several more times, and you will see that you are not only straightening the wool but also transferring much of the wool from the passive comb to the tines of the active comb. This is perfectly normal. Having these combs engage on perpendicular angles is correct and safe. NEVER leave the tines of the passive comb in the upright position. This is only to charge the wool onto the passive comb. For your safety, the combs should always be worked in a perpendicular manner to avoid impaling your hand and fingers onto the tines of the combs.

When you have combed and transferred most of the wool from the passive comb, it is time to work the wool

Figure 23. Pull locks of wool onto the comb, filling it about one-quarter of the way up.

Figure 24. Turn the comb so that the tines are facing the right if you are right-handed and toward the left if you are left-handed.

back onto the passive comb (see Figure 26). To do this, turn the active comb so that the tines are now facing toward the ceiling. Carefully swing the active comb toward the tines of the passive comb so that the wool engages and slide the fibers back against the comb's block. Continue in this manner until you have transferred most of the wool from the active comb and returned it back onto the passive comb. Comb, comb, comb back and forth until the fibers are nicely aligned (see Figure 27).

You are now ready to draw the combed fibers through a small hole in a diz (a small washer or disk with a hole in the center through which to pull the wool). This step helps to make a long length of drafted fiber that is uniform in thickness and easier to spin. Start by pulling a small amount through the hole in the diz and pinch it with the fingers of your right hand (see Figure 28). Pull on these fibers until you have several inches of fiber drawn through. The diz will move forward toward you. Push the diz back with your left hand (see Figure 29). Now pinch the wool with the fingers of your left

Figure 25. Bring the second comb down as if you are using a hammer and engage the tines of the active comb into the tip ends of the wool. Let the tines of the active comb go all the way through so the tips meet with the base of the active comb, and then pull the active comb back toward you to free it. Do this several more times.

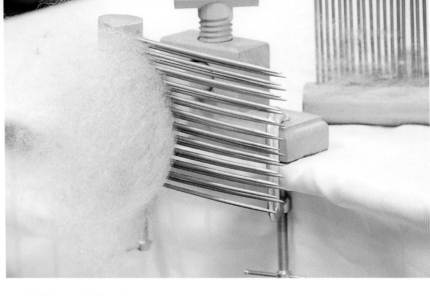

Figure 26. When you have combed and transferred most of the wool from the passive comb to the active comb, it is time to work the wool back onto the passive comb. To do this, turn the active comb so that the tines are now toward the ceiling. Carefully swing the active comb toward the tines of the passive comb so that the wool engages, and slide the fibers back against the comb's block.

hand and pull some more fiber forward. Push the diz back with your right hand and repeat the process of pinching and pulling the wool in a hand-over-hand movement (see Figure 30). Continue this way until most of the wool is removed from the comb. You will never get all the wool drawn off and through the diz. What remains is usually undesirable fiber. Pull it off the tines of the comb and discard it. If it hurts your heart to just throw it away, save it and card these fibers later. Nothing is wasted that way.

Figure 27. Repeat the combing process until the fibers are well aligned. You are now ready to pull the fibers through a small hole in a diz.

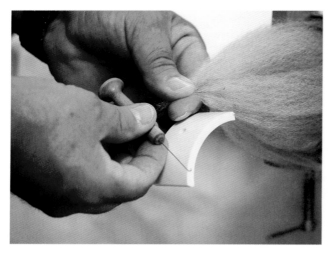

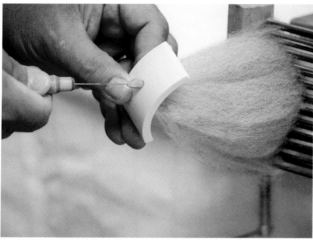
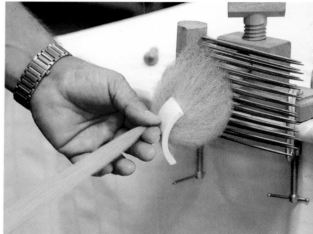

Figure 28. Pinch the fibers and start them through the hole in the diz.

Figure 29. Once you have several inches of fiber drawn through, the diz will move forward toward you. Push the diz back with your left hand.

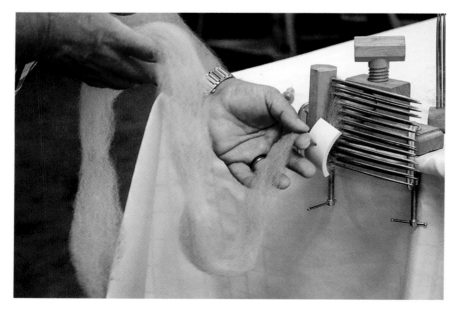

Figure 30. Then pull more fiber and push the diz back with your right hand, repeating the process of pinching and pulling the wool in a hand-over-hand movement. Continue this way until most of the wool is removed from the comb.

Flick Carding

Flick carding produces a spinning fiber that is somewhere in between carding and combing. Using a flicker brush or dog comb is one of the easiest ways to prepare wool fibers for spinning. Flick carding is easiest done with longer-stapled wool. Hold the end of a lock of wool in your hand and place it on a canvas or denim mat that you have placed on your knee (see Figure 31). Hold it tightly. Now, with the flicker or dog brush in your other hand, brush the end of the lock until it is opened up and combed out nicely. Turn the lock around, and now comb the other end (see Figure 32). Lay the locks of flick-combed wool in a basket, and when you are ready to spin, just reach for a lock of combed wool and spin it.

There are many different ways to prepare your spinning fibers. Some of these may sound a little overwhelming, but I promise you they all have merit depending on the way you want your finished thread to look and handle.

I am a visual learner. Whenever I find a new interest, I do best to find an instructor and take a class—sometimes several times, and in between I practice, practice, and practice.

If you become overwhelmed by the amount of fleece you accumulate over the years, don't despair—it has happened to me as well. I looked around and found several good carding mills in my area that were happy to help me. I simply dropped my fleeces off at the mill, and several weeks later they were all washed, carded, and made into roving and ready for me to spin. Just another way to get you spinning!

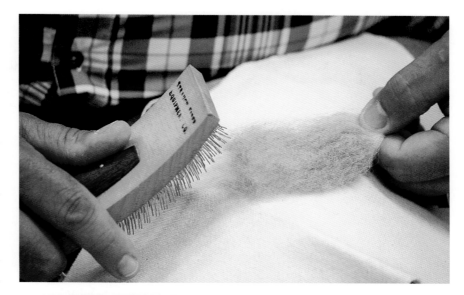

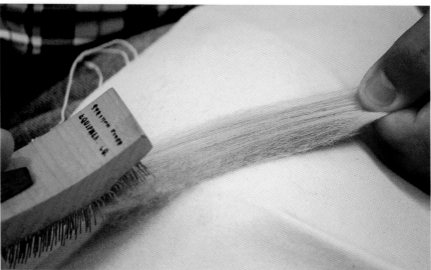

Figure 31. To flick wool, hold the end of a lock in your hand and place it on a canvas or denim mat on your knee. Hold it tightly and brush the end of the lock until it is opened up and combed out nicely.

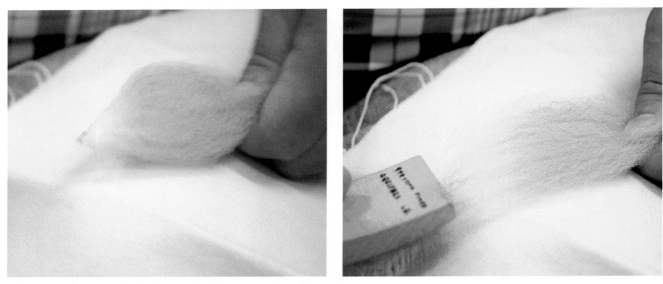

Figure 32. Then turn the lock around and repeat on the other end.

Prepared fibers

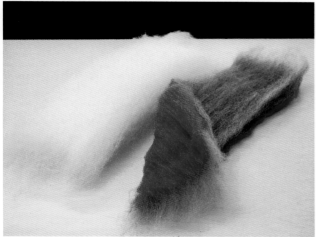

Drum carded.

Carded rolags.

Roving.

Combed.

Flicked.

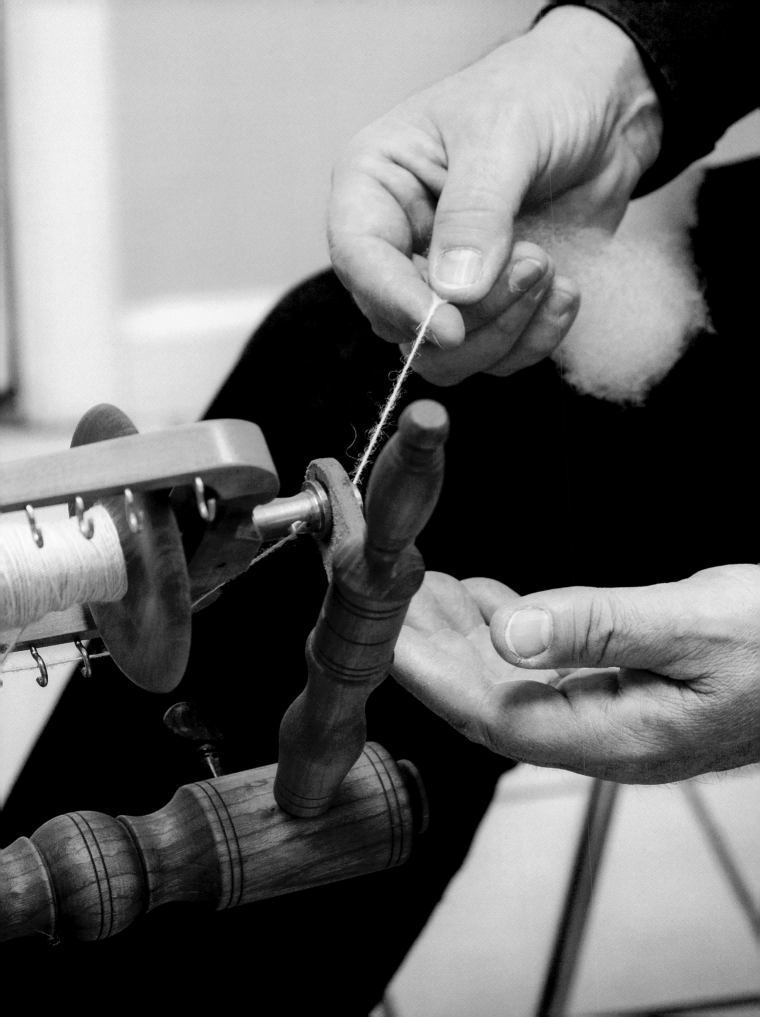

4

Spindle or Wheel?

When you are about to take the plunge and start spinning your own yarn, there are so many questions to ask: Should you start by spinning on a spindle first or just go ahead and begin on a spinning wheel? What is the best spindle or wheel, and how do you choose? If you ask twelve accomplished spinners this question, you will get a dozen different answers. I don't believe there is a correct answer, and so you need to do a little research. Better yet, take a class in which you can try spinning on spindles as well as several different spinning wheels. I feel it is personal choice. In the long run, there are no discerning qualities to a skein of yarn that indicate that it was spun on either a spindle or a wheel. It's a skein of spun yarn.

I know spinners who only spin on spindles and have many spindles in their collection. Mostly, these are for

Figure 33. Saxony wheels.

Figure 34. The pictures in stories from our childhood often depicted Saxony spinning wheels.

spinning different styles of yarn, but some spinners collect them like a form of addiction.

I also know spinners who don't enjoy spinning on a spindle and prefer to spin only on a spinning wheel or wheels. This, too, can become an addiction, and I will admit that I have had several wheels to serve different functions and some just because they are beautiful. Many are works of art. I want to stress, again, that there is no right or wrong answer as to the best equipment for you. Only you can decide what works for you, and those decisions are best made by trying different wheels. I hate to think about how many cars I have had over the years, but I would guess that I have had more spinning wheels. I would recommend that you try to find a wheel that is multifunctional and can perform any number of tasks that you ask it to do. It should spin any fiber that you want to try and be flexible enough to spin both fine and heavier-weight yarns. A sports car is fun to drive but not very practical for a young and growing family.

There are several different styles of spinning wheels. The most common styles are Saxony and Castle

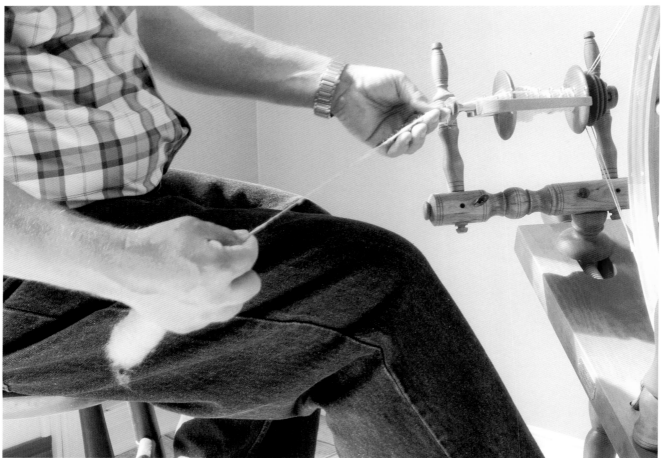

Figure 35. Saxony wheel set up for a right-handed spinner, with the flyer on the left and the wheel on the right.

Figure 36. You can find wheels made for left-handed spinners, with the wheel on the left and the flyer on the right.

wheels. The Saxony-style wheel is probably the most recognized spinning wheel (see Figures 33 and 34). This tool has been embedded in our minds since childhood. Stories like Sleeping Beauty and Rumpelstiltskin showed illustrations of Saxony-style wheels. These illustrations are not very accurate from a spinner's point of view, but they work well enough for a child to believe that a young girl pricks her finger on a spindle and falls asleep or a funny old curmudgeon is able to spin straw into gold.

As the spinner sits in front of the Saxony wheel to spin, the wheel sits off to one side, usually the right side, and the flyer is mounted off to the left side. The flyer is the mechanism that puts twist into the fiber, making it into yarn. It also winds the spun thread onto a bobbin for storage. This arrangement works well for a right-handed individual (see Figure 35). While their left hand works close to the flyer, their right hand, holding the fiber, can easily move across the spinner's lap as they draw out, or attenuate, the fibers to spin a uniform-thickness thread. There are wheel makers that offer Saxony wheels for left-handed spinners (see Figure 36). You can see how the wheel has been located on the left side and the flyer is mounted on the right. This makes it much more comfortable for the left-handed individual because they can draw the fibers out with their dominant hand (see Figure 37). If you are left-handed, be sure to investigate the possibility of trying a Saxony wheel with a left-handed orientation.

Many spinners like the look and styling of a Castle wheel (see Figure 38), and it doesn't matter if you are left- or right-handed because the flyer is mounted directly in front of you and above the wheel. A Castle-style wheel also takes up less floor space in your home (if that is a consideration). Their smaller size and footprint also make them portable for traveling. Spinning can be a solitary activity and only done at home, but I find that most spinners are very social and like to get together to spin and talk about spinning. Having a spinning wheel that fits into and travels well in your car can be a consideration. If this is an important aspect, be sure to ask the salesperson to show you how to fold and

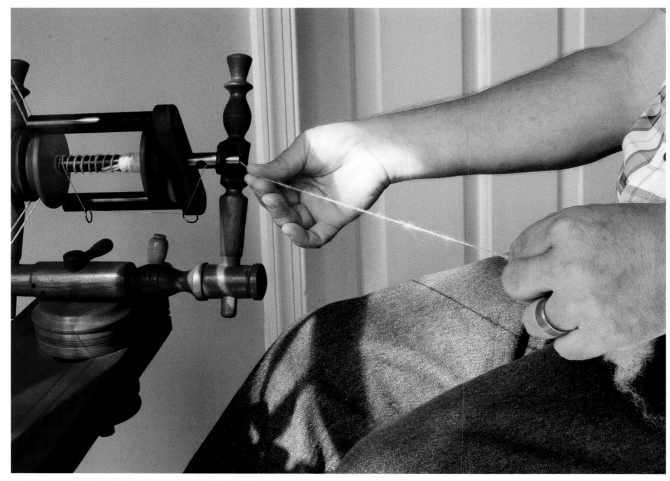

Figure 37. Left-handed spinners may hold the fiber in their left hand and pinch with their right.

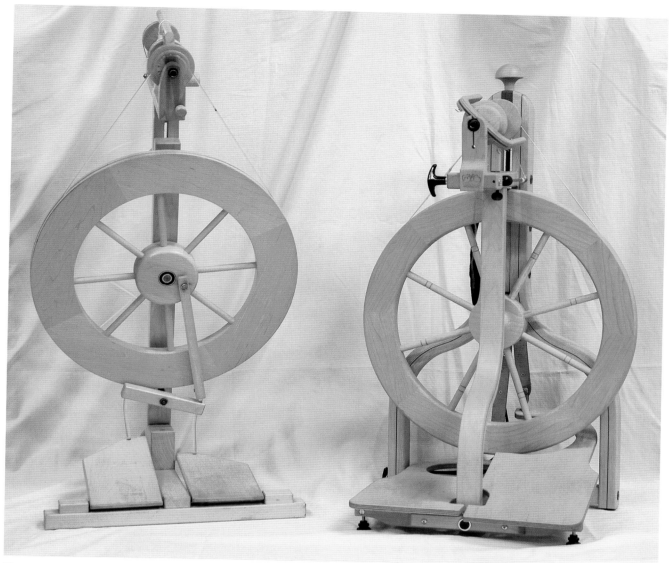

Figure 38. Castle wheels.

disassemble a wheel to make it smaller (see Figure 39). Some manufacturers even offer a protective carrying case to put your wheel in for safe travels. I have known individuals who travel for work and have bought a spinning wheel that breaks down small enough to fit in the overhead compartment of an airplane. Wow. This feature helps to eat up some long hours in a motel room and makes you productive as well.

This idea of making your spinning portable has been on the minds of spinners for thousands of years. The hand spindle was the first portable spinning tool and is still used today by many spinners all around the world, but those spinners who want a portable wheel and don't want to use a spindle are now turning to e-spinners (see Figure 40). These are an electric or battery-powered flyers that are not much larger than

a shoebox, and some are even smaller. They can travel easily and make it possible to spin almost anywhere you go. I have known spinners to spin in the passenger seat of a car to help break up a long and boring trip. The e-spinner can run off a battery or can be plugged into a port in the vehicle. Now how cool is that? It is the ultimate in portable spinning. I often wonder what my spinning ancestors would think if I could bring them back and show them my modern spinning equipment. Most likely, they wouldn't even recognize some of my wheels as spinning wheels. It would be interesting and awkward to explain the equipment to them. I might start the conversation with "Look, Grandma, an electric spinner." And her reaction might be "What's electric?"

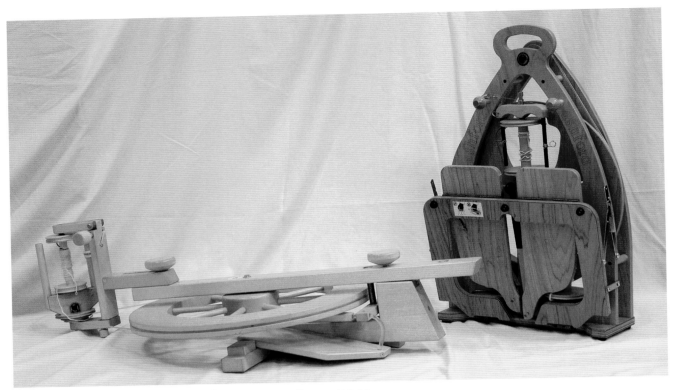

Figure 39. Some Castle wheels fold up for easy transporting or storage.

Figure 40. E-spinners run on batteries or electricity and are highly portable.

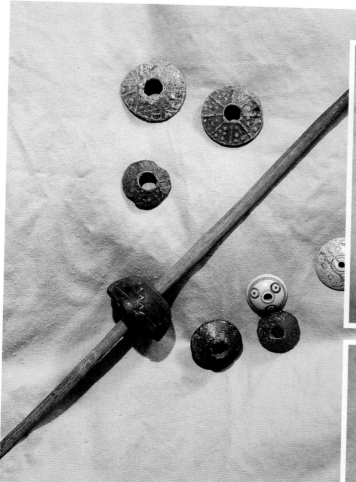

Figure 41. The earliest spinning tools were hand spindles. Ancient whorls made of fired clay, glass, bone, and other materials have been found.

Another consideration in the purchasing of a spinning wheel might be styling and aesthetics. An individual who prefers a more modern and contemporary look will not be happy with a traditional wheel. On the flip side, the person who loves interpreting spinning at a historical site will only be happy with a spinning wheel that looks appropriate to the time period. Luckily, there are spinning wheels for every taste; you just need to do a little research to find them.

In my mind, spindles are in a category all on their own. When I started spinning, the phrase associated with spindles was "drop spindles." I suppose this is because when you are just learning to use a spindle, it seems to spend a lot of time on the floor rather than in your hands—a true fact, but not one that I want to point out to a student, as I try to be encouraging as they learn to spin a continuous thread. I prefer to use the term "hand spindle" or simply "spindle."

Archeological evidence shows that people have been spinning and weaving for thousands of years. The earliest forms of spinning tools were hand spindles. These might have been as simple as a pointed stick, rolled on the thigh to put twist into fibers to make a continuous thread. At some point in time a weight, known as a whorl, was added to the stick to add momentum and to help keep the spindle going for a longer period of time. Whorls have been found made of fired clay, glass, bone, and even lead (see Figure 41). These hardened

Figure 42. A variety of spindle sizes are available. As a general rule, you will need a heavier spindle to make bulkier yarns and a lighter one for fine threads.

materials have lasted hundreds of years over time and are often found by archeologists when excavating a site.

Modern spindles can be as simple as a dowel with a wooden disk or as elaborate as a turned exotic wood shaft and whorl with brass rims. There are numerous professional spindle makers who take great pride in their work creating a spindle with a perfect balance. That balance helps to keep the spindle revolving for long periods of time and makes the task of spinning go smoothly. Depending on the materials used to make the spindle, some of these handcrafted spindles can be quite expensive compared to the ordinary, factory-produced spindle. Like the previous saying I've mentioned, "You only get as good as you pay for." That being said, it's the skill and hands of the spinner, not the price of the spindle, that make the yarn. When buying a spindle, look for one that is well balanced and that will keep revolving when given a flick of your fingers. Many show venders will encourage you to try out their spindles to see whether the balance is correct and that the spindle doesn't wobble. If you are hesitant to try a spindle yourself, ask the vender to demonstrate on the spindle you're interested in. They are more than happy to try to sell you a spindle.

If you are new to spindle spinning, I would like to make a suggestion on what to buy. Look for well-balanced spindles in a number of different weights from 2.5 oz. to 4 oz. (see Figure 42). The difference in the weight of a spindle is for spinning different size threads. A lighter-weight spindle is for finer threads, and a heavier spindle is for spinning thicker yarns. Using a heavy spindle to spin a thin yarn will often result in lots of yarn breakage during the process. The sound of your spindle hitting the floor is most discouraging. On another note, trying to spin a heavier yarn on a spindle that is too light will be difficult because the spindle will not have the correct amount of weight and momentum to keep it going.

Whether it be a spinning wheel or spindles, having the correct equipment is important. I know we have all tightened a screw with a butter knife and were quietly ashamed for not going and getting the proper screwdriver. It's a little like that with spinning equipment. Having the correct tool is important, but it doesn't need to be fancy or expensive. I have never looked at a skein of yarn and been able to identify what wheel or spindle it was spun on.

I leave you with this story: I once read an article by a spinner who took her hand-carved spindle on vacation with her. She and her family were traveling in Greece. What fun it would be, she thought, to spin with some local spinners. The tour guide said that the group would see shepherds and spinners spinning yarn and weaving fabric. The author of the article said she indeed met up with local spinners using crudely made spindles. She was so proud to show off her spindle and boast a little about its beauty. They questioned why she would travel with such a treasure and risk breaking it. "You see," someone explained, "when we are out working our sheep in the meadows, we make a spindle with a straight stick and an apple for the whorl. If we should accidently drop the spindle on the ground and the apple splits open, well, the sheep have a sweet treat." Nothing lost but much to be gained. That story appeared perhaps forty years ago, and I have never forgotten it. It makes you think, doesn't it?

Now go take a class and do some test-driving of some wheels and/or spindles. You'll be so glad you did.

Figure 43. Single-treadle Saxony wheel.

5

Parts of the Wheel

The spinning wheel is a remarkable piece of equipment made up of a number of different moving parts. Let's start getting familiar with the parts and how they function. I will start at the base of a spinning wheel and work my way up to the top.

At the bottom of the spinning wheel you will see the treadle assembly. This is where you place your foot or feet, depending on whether you have a single- or double-treadle wheel. The up-and-down motion of the treadle keeps the wheel revolving. How do you decide whether you want a single-treadle wheel or a double-treadle wheel? This has been my experience: The Saxony-style wheel works well with a single treadle (see Figure 43). At the end of the treadle, there is a wooden stick known as the footman. The footman extends upward from the treadle and is attached to the crank shaft on the drive wheel. The treadle, the footman, and the drive wheel all work in unison. It seems that the larger overall size of the drive wheel and the longer length of the footman require very little effort from the treadle to keep the action moving smoothly.

In the case of the Castle-style wheel, though, the distance between the footman and the wheel is very short because of the upright design of this style of spinning wheel. With a single treadle, it takes more effort on my foot to keep the wheel going, and it isn't as easy to treadle as it is on my Saxony wheel. One day I sat at a Castle wheel that had double treadles. The action was much like riding a bicycle, and the wheel spun smoothly and with very little effort. The required energy to make the wheel go around was now split between my two feet. At that point my mind was sold on the idea of double treadles for Castle-style wheels.

This is definitely something to consider when buying your first wheel. A single treadle will work fine on a Saxony wheel, but choose double treadles for a Castle wheel (see Figure 44).

The size of the drive wheel is another consideration. Castle-style wheels tend to have smaller drive wheels. Their diameter typically measures somewhere between 16 and 20 inches. This is more than adequate and keeps them small enough to still consider them portable.

Figure 44. For a Castle wheel, having two treadles is best.

Figure 45. Wheels with a 30-inch diameter such as these by Norman Hall (left) and the Schacht Reeves Production Wheel (right) spin very fast. They make yarn quickly but may spin too fast for a new spinner.

Saxony-style wheels tend to have larger drive wheels, with diameters of 20–24 inches. The momentum of these large wheels keeps the spinning action going smoothly. There are Saxony wheels with even larger diameters. The diameter of the Saxony wheel by Norman Hall and the Schacht Reeves Production Wheel is 30 inches (see Figure 45). Like other wheels with this larger-size diameter, these are considered production wheels, and they spin very fast. The spinner needs only to treadle slowly to keep these wheels going. This is sometime difficult the first time spinning on a production wheel. The wheel can quickly get away from a spinner with a set muscle memory and rhythm. Like anything you do, it takes a little practice at first.

There is a drive band that goes around the rim of the drive wheel and travels to and around the flyer. The flyer is where all the magic happens (see Figure 46). It functions

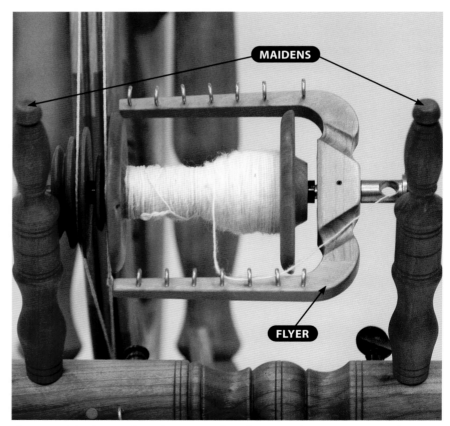

Figure 46. The flyer is where the action takes place; it sits between two upright posts called the maidens.

WHORL

BOBBIN

MOTHER OF ALL

Figure 47. The maidens are held by the Mother of All.

to put the needed twist into the fiber, in addition to drawing the newly made yarn onto a bobbin for storage. The flyer is mounted between two points known as the maidens. The maidens are held by the Mother of All (see Figure 47) (I know what you're thinking, and I promise you that I am not making this up; these are names that were given to these parts hundreds of years ago and are still used today). The flyer is made up of several different parts. There is a bobbin that rotates freely on the center shaft of the flyer. At one end of the flyer, there is a disk called the whorl. The whorl has several different grooves cut to different depths and circumferences. These grooves determine the rotational speed of the flyer, or the ratios of the flyer. If the flyer spins 12 times to one rotational turn of the wheel, well, then it is considered a 12:1 ratio. Think about the whorl like the gears on a bicycle. The largest grooves slow the speed of the flyer, and the smallest groove speeds up the flyer. The slowest speed is used for yarns needing a softer twist. For threads requiring a tighter

Figure 48. The arms of the flyer will have either hooks or a sliding ring to guide the newly spun yarn onto the bobbin. You will need to move the sliding ring or change to a different hook throughout the process to wind the yarn on the bobbin evenly.

Figure 49. Make sure your drive cords (or bands) are smooth, with no noticeable bumps.

Flyers operate in three different ways: double drive, Scotch tension, and bobbin lead or Irish tension.

Double-drive spinning wheels use a long length of cord that travels around the wheel and whorl twice. The cord is either tied with a knot or sewn together so that it has a smooth join. You don't want to feel a noticeable bump each time the knot goes around the grooves of the whorl or bobbin (see Figure 49). One band travels around the bobbin and the other band goes over a groove on the whorl. Both bands go over and around the drive wheel. Tension can be applied to the drive band with a tension knob (see Figure 50). This is often located at the end of the wheel's table or

TENSION KNOB

Figure 50. The tension knob is often located at the end of the wheel's table or near or on the Mother of All. Turn the tension knob to tighten or loosen the drive band.

twist, you might want to go to a faster speed or ratio for spinning shorter-length fibers such as cotton. Cotton requires more twist to the thread to make it hold together so that it doesn't drift apart. You will notice that there are two arms on the flyer with either hooks or a sliding ring that guides the newly spun yarn onto the bobbin (see Figure 48). Throughout the spinning process, you will need to move the sliding ring or change to a different hook to wind the yarn on the bobbin evenly. If you have a flyer with a self-winding mechanism, the guide ring traverses forward and backward over the bobbin, and you get a very evenly wound bobbin.

Figure 51. Scotch-tensioned spinning wheels also have a brake band, tensioned separately, with a spring or rubber band on one end to allow some flexibility.

on/around the Mother of All. Turn the tension knob in both directions so that you can see how it works to either tighten the drive band or loosen it.

Scotch-tensioned spinning wheels work slightly differently. They still require a drive band going over the whorl. This can be a linen or cotton cord or a flexible polypropylene band. Spinners love this flexible drive band because it adjusts easily to the different-sized grooves on the whorl. There still is, in many cases, a means to tighten or loosen the drive band. Each spinning wheel manufacturer has its own design on how to do this. A separate cord travels around and goes over the bobbin. This is known as the brake band (see Figure 51). This cord is tensioned separately. On one end of the brake band, there is a spring or rubber band to allow some flexibility. On the other end of the brake

Figure 52. The brake band is attached to a tensioning knob that can be tightened or loosened to control the speed at which the spun yarn is being drawn onto the bobbin.

band is a tensioning knob (see Figure 52). This tensioning knob controls the speed at which the spun yarn is being drawn onto the bobbin. When the brake band is loosened, the yarn remains in the spinner's hand for a longer time and allows the twist to become greater. This is sometimes wanted, such as when you are spinning cotton. If the brake band is tightened, the yarn is drawn onto the bobbin more quickly. It takes a little playing with until you find just the right amount of tension on the brake band. I like to think of it in this way: Pretend you are adjusting the tuning key on a violin or cello. You turn the key to tighten or loosen the string to achieve just the right pitch. The brake band knob is the same.

Bobbin-lead or Irish-tensioned spinning wheels work in the opposite configuration of the Scotch-tensioned wheel. With a bobbin-lead wheel, the drive band goes directly over the bobbin (see Figure 53). The flyer speed is controlled with a leather thong or strap that goes over the orifice end of the flyer (see Figure 54). A tension knob applies pressure onto the strap and controls the speed at which the flyer turns (and hence the amount of twist put into the yarn).

I hope this clearly explains the different parts of a spinning wheel. I promise that you will find all kinds of variations of these parts, depending on the style and manufacturer. Choosing a spinning wheel is a personal matter. I have more than one knife in my kitchen. It's not unheard of to have more than one wheel. Each one has its own unique job to do.

Many spinning-wheel makers offer the option of having their wheel work as either a double-drive wheel or

Figure 53. With a bobbin-lead (also known as Irish-tensioned) wheel, the drive band goes directly over the bobbin.

a Scotch-tensioned wheel. This is a good marketing move for the makers of spinning wheels. The owners can choose whichever way works best for them. I don't know of a single spinner who changes back and forth between the two systems based on what fiber they are spinning at the time. I do know for sure that I personally have a better time spinning cotton on a Scotch-tensioned setup, because I can reduce the drag on the brake band while putting a high twist in the thread. Since cotton relies on a lot of twist for strength, I can hold back on the thread and let the twist build up before letting the thread wind onto the bobbin. If you are looking for a wheel that can spin a bulky-weight thread with a softer twist, you can't go wrong with a bobbin-lead wheel. The maker Louët leads the market for bobbin-lead wheels.

Figure 54. The flyer speed on a bobbin-lead wheel is controlled with a leather strap that goes over the orifice end of the flyer.

6

Let's Start Spinning

So let's get started spinning. Look around you to see that you have everything you will need. Do you have your prepared fiber? I like starting my students with a medium-grade wool fiber like you get with Corriedale or Romney sheep. Have you oiled and lubricated the moving parts of your wheel? I pay particular attention to the flyer and bobbin because it's the flyer that's applying the twist and winding the thread onto the bobbin. The flyer needs to run easily, and a few drops of oil will keep the flyer moving freely. If neglected, the flyer will turn sluggishly and may be noisy and squeak back at you. I also put a few drops of oil on the crankshaft and treadle assembly before I get started.

Treadle at first with no wool to get comfortable with treadling action. This is sometimes the hardest part of spinning. Keeping the wheel going in the same direction constantly has proven to be a challenge for many beginning spinners. Sometimes the wheel wants to go backward on you. This is perfectly normal and, I know, frustrating. Keep practicing to maintain the wheel turning in a *clockwise* direction. Try to maintain a smooth waltz rhythm: 1-2-3, 1-2-3, 1-2-3. Your toe will go down on 1 and come up on the 3. Since spinning requires your hands and feet to work together, try this to practice: Sit at your wheel and just treadle to keep your wheel rotating clockwise to an even rhythm. When you think you have it, pick up some handwork such as knitting or a fleece to pick to open the locks, but keep treadling. This approach will give your hands something to do, and you will soon forget about the treadling. The treadling will become second nature to you. This is what you need to do to become comfortable with the spinning process. When your feet are working independently on their own and separately from your hands, well, then, you can concentrate on what your hands need to be doing.

If you are starting off with a brand-new spinning wheel, you will also have bare bobbins. You will need to add a leader onto the bobbins to get started. A leader is the connection between the bobbin and the spinning fiber. I like using a length of cotton cord that's about two yards long. I tie the two ends together to make a loop (see Figure 55). This is the leader. To attach the leader to the bobbin, pass the leader under the bobbin shaft and pass the loop end through the knot end. Pull up on the loop end until the knot end is snug against

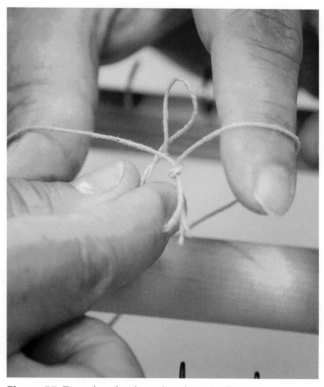

Figure 55. To make a leader, take a length of cotton cord about two yards long and tie the ends together to make a loop.

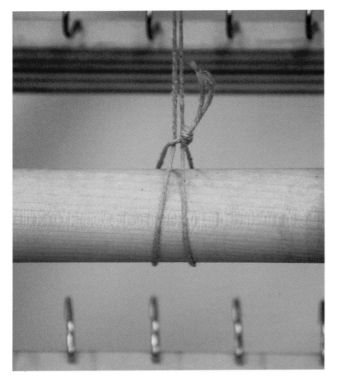

Figure 56. Pass the leader under the bobbin shaft and pass the loop end through the knot end. Pull up on the loop end until the knot end is snug against the bobbin shaft.

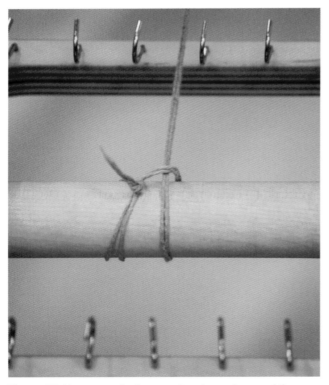

Figure 57. Now wrap the loop end under and around the bobbin shaft again and pass it through itself (half hitch knot). Your leader is ready to use.

the bobbin shaft (see Figure 56). Now, wrap the loop end under and around the bobbin shaft again and pass it through itself (see Figure 57). This is known as a half hitch knot. The leader, once attached to the bobbin, will last a very long time.

Pass the leader through the guide ring, or, if your flyer has guide hooks, pass the leader over the first guide hook on the flyer. Using a threading hook, pass the hook into the orifice opening and catch the leader end and pull it through and out of the orifice (see Figure 58). The looped end of the leader is what you will use to catch and attach your spinning fiber (see Figure 59).

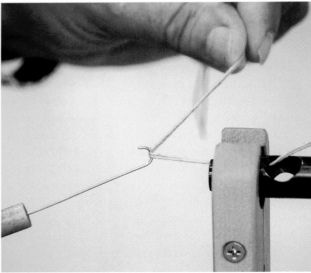

Figure 58. Pass the leader through the guide ring or first hook on the flyer, and use a threading hook to pull it through the orifice.

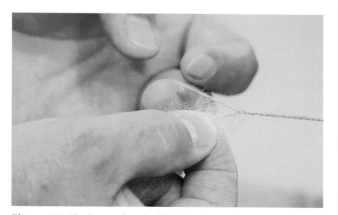

Figure 59. The looped end of the leader is what you will use to catch and attach your spinning fiber.

If you are using a wheel with a double-drive assembly, take a moment to see that the drive bands are correctly going over the bobbin groove and whorl (see Figure 60). If you are using a wheel with Scotch tension, be sure that the drive band is going over the whorl and the brake band is correctly passing over the bobbin (see Figure 61). Adjust and tighten any bands so that they are not loose and coming off when you treadle the wheel. Tension knobs will need to be adjusted during the spinning process to the discretion of the spinner depending on how quickly you want the newly spun thread to be taken up onto the bobbin. That is the reason for the tension knobs. They control the speed at which the spun yarn is drawn onto the bobbin.

Figure 60. On a double-drive wheel, make sure that the drive bands are going correctly over the bobbin groove and whorl.

Figure 61. On a wheel with Scotch tension, be sure that the drive band is going over the whorl and the brake band is correctly passing over the bobbin.

Short Draw

Let's start with a technique called spinning with a short draw. This is the preferred method for spinning worsted-spun yarns. Place a small amount of wool fiber into the loop end of your leader (see Figure 62). Treadle with the wheel going clockwise, and you will see the leader start to twist and tighten up, trapping the wool fibers in the loop. Tighten the drive band or brake band so the leader is just barely pulling in. It's an awkward feeling at first. The drawing of the leader is somewhat like the pull of a retractable cord on an appliance.

I am right-handed. I hold my prepared fiber in this hand. I don't hold a lot of fiber in my hand at one time. When spinning from roving, I tear off about 6–8 inches of roving. This is more than enough to comfortably hold in my hand at one time. My left hand pinches a small amount of fiber between my index and middle finger and thumb (see Figure 63). My right hand holds the fiber with a little bit of resistance while my left hand pushes the fibers toward the orifice (see Figure 64). The distance between my left hand and right hand is known as the drafting zone. The amount of fiber in the drafting zone determines the thickness of the yarn. The more fiber in the drafting zone, the thicker the yarn will be. Smaller amounts will result

Figure 62. Place a small amount of fiber into the loop end of your leader and begin to treadle with the wheel going clockwise. Twist will begin to go into your leader and work its way to the fiber in your hand and start to pull.

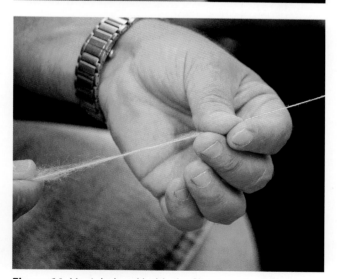

Figure 64. My right hand holds the fiber loosely, allowing more to be drawn out as my left hand pushes forward. The fiber between my hands is in the drafting zone. As you pull out with your left hand, the amount of fiber in the drafting zone is what will become your yarn. This is where you control the thickness of your yarn.

Figure 63. My left hand pinches the fiber between my index finger and thumb and will control the amount of twist going into the yarn.

in a thinner yarn. The left hand controls the twist being put into that thread. The left hand pinches the fibers and moves them forward and away from the fiber source until the desired amount of fiber is shown in the drafting zone. The fingers of my left hand then move back toward the right hand, guiding the twist. Do not allow the twist to get behind your fingers and lock up the drafting zone. Always keep the twist in front of the fingers of your left hand. When the left and right hands come together, pinch another small amount of fiber from the fiber source and continue as described. There is no recommended or set distance that your hands separate as you draft the fibers. This is often based on the staple length of the wool.

As you spin, the yarn will be pulled onto and stored on the bobbin. The bobbin fills quickly, and it's best to move the guide or stop and move the yarn onto a different guide hook (see Figure 65). This helps to fill the bobbin evenly as the yarn builds up on the shaft of the bobbin. As you spin and fill the bobbin, it's likely you will need to make adjustments to the take up and tighten the tension knob. If you experience a slowing down of the draw or it doesn't feel like the yarn is being wound onto the bobbin, stop and look first to see whether the yarn is caught on a hook. If the yarn is smoothly moving over the guide but just moving slowly, tighten the tension knob until the yarn is moving again at the same rate as before.

You want to check from time to time to see that you are getting sufficient twist in your thread to allow you to ply it later on. Too little twist in the singles, and the

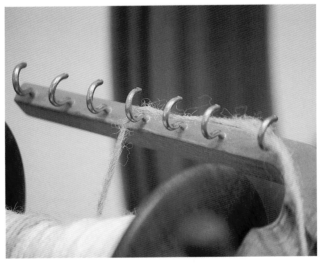

Figure 65. As you spin, the yarn will be pulled onto the bobbin. The bobbin fills quickly, and you will need to move the guide or stop and move the yarn onto a different yarn hook.

Helpful Hints for the New Spinner

1. If you are having trouble keeping the wheel going in the same direction, practice treadling all by itself. Each wheel has a different feel to its treadling. To get accustomed to the feel of your wheel, sit at the wheel and place your foot on the treadle and turn the wheel with your hand clockwise. Feel the treadle go up and down under your foot? Now practice treadling with a slow rhythm to keep it going. Once it is going, sit for some time and just treadle on its own. Later, try doing something with your hands to simulate the action of spinning yarn and treadling at the same time. If you are a knitter, try knitting and treadling at the same time. See what I mean? It's like patting your head and rubbing your tummy at the same time. That's what the spinning process is like: doing two things at the same time. Getting the correct rhythm takes practice.

2. Another common problem for beginners is getting the correct draw of the thread onto the bobbin. Start by having very little draw on your thread at first, and then turn the tension knob until you feel the spun yarn being pulled onto the bobbin. It should be gentle and consistent. Don't let it pull too hard at first and rip the thread and fiber out of your hand. If you are experiencing a lot of breakage of your yarn, it might be that the tension is too high and needs to be loosened. Make small adjustments to the tension knob. I think it is a lot like adjusting the strings on a musical instrument. Make small turns to the knob to obtain just the correct sound. Or, in your case, the right draw of your thread.

strands won't ply. Too much twist in the singles will make for a very firm plied yarn. I like to start out by spinning a few yards of single-spun yarn, and then I stop the wheel. Next, I pull about 12–14 inches of yarn off the bobbin by unwinding the thread off the bobbin and pulling it out through the flyer's orifice toward me. Let the yarn naturally twist back on itself and look at what would be the yarn if it were plied at this point. Does it look like a yarn that you would be happy with?

If not, adjust the tension knob to increase or decrease the amount of draw onto the bobbin, or perhaps also adjust the whorl ratio to a faster or slower speed at this point. Don't be afraid to play with the adjustments to get the results you want.

I like to spin until the yarn reaches the top of the flanges of the bobbin. You are now ready to remove the bobbin from the flyer and replace it with an empty bobbin and repeat the process. This is a good time to see whether the flyer needs to be oiled again. If the flyer shaft is dry, put a few drops of oil onto the length of the metal shaft. Replace the bobbin and return the flyer to the Mother of All and reassemble the wheel and adjust the tension on the drive band.

Long Draw

When spinning with the long draw technique, the left hand stays a few inches away from the orifice (see Figure 66). The fingers of the left hand pinch the twist tightly while the right hand, which is holding the fiber, pulls back slowly, stretching the fibers into a thin wisp (see Figure 67). To prevent the stretched fibers from breaking or drifting apart, the fingers of the left hand release a small amount of the twist, allowing it to enter the drafted area of fiber, giving it strength and stability. The fingers of the left hand then pinch again to trap the twist. The spinner pulls out more fiber while, again, the twist is slowly released. Like a rhythmical dance between the hands, the spinner drafts and releases twist until the spinner has drafted a comfortable length of yarn. This might be 30–36 inches of yarn. At this point, the spinner gently releases the fingers on their left hand and watches the twist travel up the length of newly formed yarn. When the spinner has enough twist placed in the thread, they move their right hand toward the wheel's orifice. The left hand takes over again by pinching the yarn and the spinner drafts out another length of yarn. The long draw takes practice, but once perfected, it is a faster way of spinning yarn. The long draw is used for making softly spun yarn with a lofty appearance. This is known as a woolen-spun yarn. Many knitting yarns are woolen spun.

Whatever method you choose to spin, remember to adjust your drive band tensions and move the thread guides for an evenly filled bobbin. When you have two full bobbins of single-spun yarn, you will now be ready to ply them together. This will help to even out the energy building up in the single twisted thread.

Figure 66. When spinning with the long draw technique, the left hand stays a few inches away from the orifice. The fingers of the left hand pinch the twist tightly while the right hand, which is holding the fiber, pulls back slowly, stretching the fibers into a thin wisp.

Figure 67. The fingers of the left hand release a small amount of the twist, allowing it to enter the drafted area of fiber, and then pinch again to trap the twist. The spinner pulls out more fiber while, again, the twist is slowly released. The spinner drafts and releases the twist until they have drafted 30–36 inches of yarn. At this point, the spinner gently releases the fingers on their left hand and watches the twist travel up the length of newly formed yarn.

Spindle Spinning

Although many spinners start off spinning on a wheel, many people start their adventure with a spindle. This may be for a number of reasons. One good reason is its smaller size and portability. You can take it anywhere that you think you might get a moment to spin a few yards of thread, such as your lunchtime break or waiting at a bus stop. The other major consideration is the price to get started. Spindles are relatively inexpensive.

There are several different styles of spindles: the high whorl, the low whorl, and the Turkish, just to name a few (see Figure 68). When looking for your first spindle, there are a few things to look for. Your spindle needs to have good balance so that it spins smoothly without a wobble. It should turn like a spinning top. Spindles are chosen by their weight. This determines what size yarn you will spin. A lighter-weight spindle is generally used for spinning fine threads. A heavy-weight spindle is for spinning heavy yarns, such as rug yarns, or for plying yarns. I would

recommend that you start with a medium-weight spindle between three and four ounces. I like a high-whorl spindle for its ease and balance (Figure 69). You will notice that it has a shaft located below the spindle whorl and a small hook just above the whorl. The shaft is turned by your hand to get the spindle started. The hook at the top centers the thread being spun (see Figure 70). When a comfortable length of yarn has been spun, the newly spun yarn is wound and stored on the spindle shaft just below the spindle's whorl.

To get started, have a small amount of prepared fiber ready to go. You can add a leader to your spindle like the one described earlier for your spinning wheel, or you can simply place a small amount of fiber under the spindle's hook (see Figure 71). Turn the spindle clockwise with your free hand until it twists the fibers together. With the fibers tightly twisted and locked around the hook, gently pull against the spindle to create a drafting zone. Allow some of the twist to

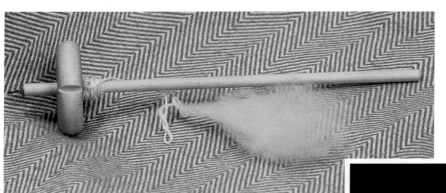

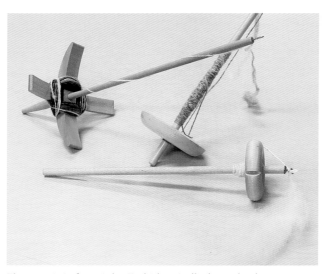

Figure 69. I like a high-whorl spindle. You will notice it has a shaft located below the spindle whorl and a small hook just above the whorl. The shaft is turned by hand to get it started.

Figure 68. Left to right: Turkish spindle, low whorl, high whorl.

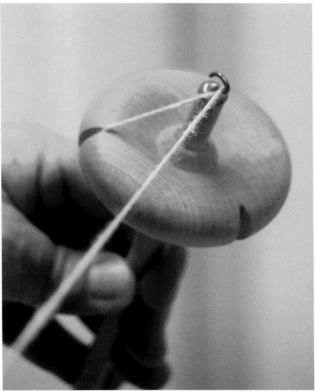

Figure 70. The hook at the top centers the yarn being spun. When a length of yarn has been spun, the newly spun yarn is wound on the spindle shaft just below the whorl.

Figure 71. To begin spinning, attach fibers to the hook directly or with a leader, and turn the spindle clockwise until it twists the fibers together. Gently pull against the spindle to create a drafting zone, and allow some of the twist into the drafting zone. Continue drafting and spinning the spindle, pinching off the twist and then allowing it in, similar to the short draw method described for spinning on a spinning wheel.

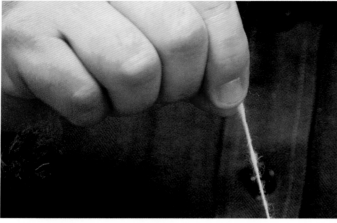

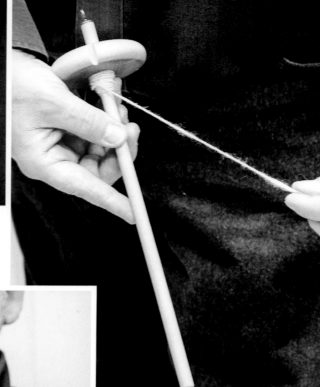

Figure 72. To wind your yarn onto the spindle shaft, hold the spindle in one hand and pinch the end of the thread, and then carefully release the yarn from the hook and wrap it around the shaft.

Figure 73. Allow 12–14 inches of yarn to remain as you reattach the yarn under the hook.

Figure 74. Pass the yarn under the hook coming from the left side of the hook. Wrap once or twice to secure the thread, and you are ready to resume spinning.

travel up into the drafting zone to start your thread. Now add some more twist by turning the spindle clockwise. With the spindle turning, draft and spin as described in the explanation for the short draw on a spinning wheel (see page 61). Draft and spin, draft and spin. The action is much like stretching a piece of dough between your hands, all the while allowing the twist to be entered into the thread to give it strength. Be sure the spindle continues to spin. If it stops, it will reverse and go in a counterclockwise direction and remove the twist.

When you have spun a comfortable length of thread, 30–36 inches long, it is time to wind the thread onto the spindle shaft (see Figure 72). Hold the spindle in one hand and pinch the end of the thread. Carefully

release the thread from the hook and wrap the thread around the shaft. Allow 12–14 inches of this thread to remain as you reattach the thread under the hook (see Figure 73). Pass the thread under the hook coming from the left side of the hook (see Figure 74). Wrap once or twice to secure the thread. You are now ready to resume spinning. With a quick flick of your fingers, turn the spindle clockwise with your free hand and continue spinning. When the spindle is full, wind the newly spun thread into a ball of yarn and set it aside. Now spin a second spindle full and again wind it into a ball. It is from these two balls of yarn that you will learn to ply. To even out the twist in your yarn, you'll need to ply them together. The resulting 2-ply yarn will be balanced and ready to use.

7

Plying

Plying is the twisting of two or more single-spun yarns together. The singles are twisted in the opposite direction of what they were originally spun. The reason for doing this is to balance the yarn so that it is not overspun or overtwisted. You may also wish to ply a heavier-weight yarn by plying multiple strands together. When the wheel or spindle is turned in the opposite direction, the energized yarns release some of the twist, and the yarns are said to be balanced.

A single yarn is usually spun by turning the wheel or spindle in a clockwise direction. This puts a Z-twist into the yarn. It can be recognized by the sloping angle in the yarn's twist—somewhat like the angle drawn in the letter Z. In the process of spinning a yarn, it is not unusual to get some overtwist. It's necessary to add strength and stability to the yarn. If you stop your

wheel and relax the thread just a little, you will notice it kinking back on itself (see Figure 75). This occurrence is not only normal but also necessary to be able to ply your yarn later. If your singles yarn doesn't kink back on itself, it is too softly spun and lacks the energy it will take to ply later. A softly spun singles yarn will fall apart when you attempt to ply it.

To ply the Z-spun singles, you will need to ply two or more yarns together. These yarns are described as 2-ply, 3-ply, or 4-ply yarn. Don't know what ply your yarn is? Take any yarn and untwist the end. Individual strands will become apparent, and you can easily count them. Figure 76 shows an example of a 4-ply thread.

When I ply my yarns, I usually make a 2-ply yarn. This suits all my needs. So why is there a need for 3- and 4-ply yarns? Are they just thicker? The answer

Figure 75. If you pull a bit of your yarn back off the bobbin while spinning, you will notice it kinking back on itself. This is normal and will give you an idea of what your yarn will be like when plied. If it doesn't kink back on itself, it is too softly spun and will easily fall apart.

Figure 76. By untwisting a yarn, you can count its plies. This is a 4-ply yarn.

Figure 77. Worsted-weight yarn in 4-ply.

is NO. The number of plies has nothing to do with the weight of the yarn. There are 2-ply yarns that are as thick as your finger and 4-ply threads as fine as a human hair. A lot depends on the size of the singles. You can easily see this with any yarn. If you double it, as if you were making a 2-ply thread, it will be twice the size. Three strands twisted together will make it even heavier, and so forth. Let's look at a photo of a 4-ply worsted-weight yarn (see Figure 77). I have untwisted the end so that you can see the 4 individual strands. Its manufacturer says it has 800 yards to the pound. That means that just one of the fine single-strand yarns was spun to a weight with 3,200 yards to the pound. If this same singles was doubled and made into a 2-ply yarn, it would have 1,600 yards to the pound. Double it again, and you now have a 4-ply with 800 yards per pound. Worsted-weight yarn in 4-ply is very common and used by many knitters. It's a staple in any knitter's stash of yarn. Now, if you want to spin your own version with the 4-ply twist, you will need to spin a rather fine singles to accomplish this. What's different about a 4-ply? Couldn't you just spin a heavy 2-ply yarn with 800 yards per pound? Will it still be a worsted weight, but with fewer plies? That is correct.

One day, many years ago, I had what can only be described as an epiphany. I worked for the well-known studio The Mannings Handweaving School and Supply Center. We carried threads and yarns for both weaving and knitting. The weaving threads were finer in comparison to the knitting yarns and had sizes such as 3/2, 5/2, 8/2, 10/2, and so forth. The first number refers to the size of the singles, and the second number tells you the number of plies. The knitting yarn sizes were DK weight, Aran weight, Shetland weight, and the famous worsted weight. Nearly all were either 3- or 4-ply yarn. So why the need for multiple plies? The answer I came to discover was this: The architectures of woven and knitted fabrics are very different in their construction. A woven cloth is made of horizontal and vertical planes of thread that intersect with each other at different spots. A 2-ply thread, when magnified, has a serrated edge that resembles the edge of a bread knife. These high-low areas seem to snuggle into each other at these intersections and weave a sound, smooth cloth. A knitted fabric is constructed on round needles. Loops of yarn, made on these round needles, intersect through each other in consecutive row after consecutive row. To my eye, the rounder the thread, the more defined the knitted stitch is.

So, just for fun, look at a 2-ply thread under magnification, and you will see the serrated edge with its high and low areas along the length of the thread. Then take a pair of scissors and cut a piece of 4-ply yarn and look at the end straight on. It's round. This explained why I preferred to use 2-ply yarns in my woven pieces. The surface area of a rounder yarn just didn't seem to weave as tightly.

The choice is yours when designing your own yarns. Sample, sample, sample before you make a garment's worth of yarn.

Plying on a Wheel

When using a spinning wheel, start with a clean bobbin and leader on your flyer. Thread the leader over the guide hooks and out through the orifice. Place your filled bobbins on a Lazy Kate (see Figure 78). The Lazy Kate is a separate tool used to hold your bobbins while you ply your yarns. I like to place my Kate on my right side and behind me on a table or on the floor. Place the ends of your yarn through the leader's loop and fold them back (see Figure 79). Start your wheel in a *counterclockwise* direction. You will see the leader and yarns start to twist in an S-twist direction

Figure 78. Lazy Kate.

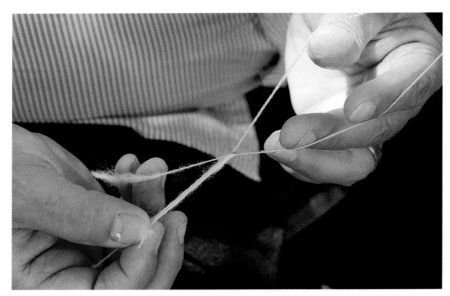

Figure 79. To start plying, place the ends of your two singles through the loop of the leader and fold them back.

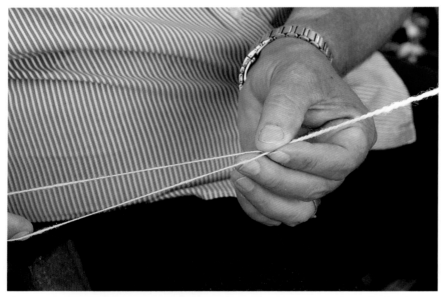

Figure 80. Start your wheel in a *counterclockwise* direction. You will see the leader and yarn start to twist in an S-twist direction.

(see Figure 80). Place the index finger of your right hand between the two yarns to separate them (see Figure 81). Place your right hand in your lap while your left hand guides the twist up the length of your thread. The action is much like when you are spinning. Pinch the yarns in front of the right hand and draft them forward toward the orifice. Then guide the twist back and pinch again. Count the drafting action much like you did when spinning the singles yarn: 1-2-3. The bobbin fills up quickly, so remember to change to different hooks as you ply your yarns.

In the process of plying, sometimes you come across a weak spot in one of the singles. If it breaks during plying, don't panic. It happens to all of us. It could happen as a result of a softly spun area that drifts apart, or it could be a thin spot and it just breaks. When this happens, stop the treadling and stop the wheel (see Figure 82). Take a moment to overlap the broken ends. It's as if you are making a splice. Slowly start treadling again. The other, nonaffected strand will wrap around and ply over the splice, making the yarn strong and the break nearly undetectable (see Figure 83). Any loose ends can be trimmed if you would like.

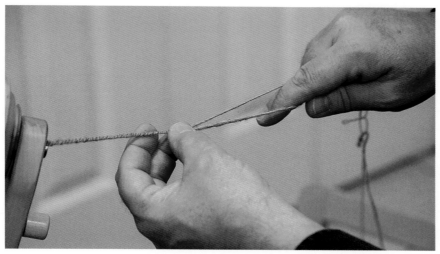

Figure 81. Place the index finger of your right hand between the two yarns to separate them, and use an action much like spinning to allow twist to ply the singles together.

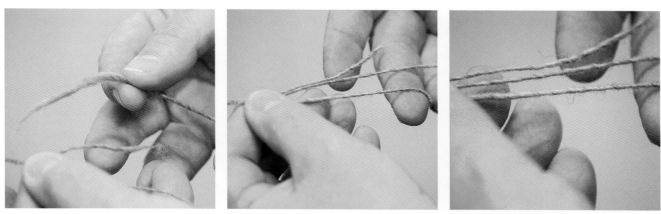

Figure 82. If (when) one of your singles breaks during plying, stop the wheel, overlap the broken ends, and slowly start treadling again, pulling the broken end back into the twist.

Figure 83. The splice will be nearly undetectable in the finished yarn.

Plying on a Spindle

If you are using a spindle, the process is much the same as spinning on a wheel. You want to attach the ends to the spindle shaft and then bring them up and over the ridge of the spindle whorl. Hook the two strands of yarn around the hook at the top of the whorl. Pass the yarns to the left of the hook and go around the hook to secure them. Now turn the spindle counterclockwise. You will see the two yarns twist together in an S-twist direction. Guide the twist along the length of the thread for a distance of 30–40 inches. Pinch the yarns with your right hand to stop the twist going any farther. With your left hand, undo the newly plied yarn from the hook and start to wrap it around the spindle shaft to store it. Leaving about 12–14 inches of yarn unwound, reattach the yarn by wrapping it on the hook by going around it again from the left. This will hold it from coming loose. If you wrap it from the right side, it will come undone as the spindle turns counterclockwise.

Spindle spinners often work from two balls of Z-spun singles, while wheel spinners work from bobbins. That is not to say that a wheel spinner couldn't use two balls of yarn to ply their yarn. They certainly could and often do when using an antique wheel that only has one bobbin on the flyer. Since you don't have additional bobbins to work from, you must unwind the singles yarn from the bobbin; then, when you have two balls, you ply from the balls onto the bobbin. You may wind balls by hand, or ball winders may be used (see Figure 84). When the ball is removed from the ball winder, you have two sources to work from: the center of the ball and the outside end of the ball. If you take the two ends and ply your thread from the center and the outside of the ball, when you reach the end, you are finished. When working from two balls (or two bobbins) of yarn, it is unlikely that you will have the same amount of yarn on both balls. One ball of singles will run out before the other ball, and you will have several yards remaining from the second ball of yarn. This material can be incorporated into the next length of yarn you ply.

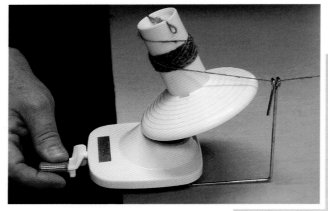

Figure 84. Ball winder.

Helpful hint for plying from balls of yarn:
Try making a containment field that keeps the balls of yarn from rolling all over the floor. Two bowls or crocks will do the trick nicely. I like using two clean flowerpots turned upside down—I place the balls under the pots and bring the single strands up through the holes in the pots. Empty tissue boxes also work very well.

Make a Skein

When you are finished plying your yarns, you will want to unwind them from the bobbin and make a skein. This is best done on a skein winder or a niddy noddy (see Figures 85 and 86). When using a skein winder, you simply tie the loose end of thread to the handle of the skein winder and turn the handle clockwise. The yarn will wind around the arms of the winder. The circumference of the winder arms can differ. Many are between 60 inches and 72 inches for two yards. When you are finished winding the yarn off the bobbin, count the wraps and multiply the wraps by the number of inches that your winder has in its circumference. This will give you the total number of inches. Then divide the inches by 36, and you will have the number of yards you have plied.

Figure 85. Skein winder.

Figure 86.
Niddy noddy.

The niddy noddy works the same way. Many niddy noddies are 2 yards for one complete pass around. Start by holding the end of the yarn against the center post. Now wind it on the outside arms of the niddy noddy, following the illustration (see Figure 87).

When you are finished winding your yarn into a skein, it is time to secure it with a couple of string ties. First, tie the two ends of the skein together. This is the beginning end to the finished end. If the two ends are not meeting at the same location, simply back off a few inches until they meet at the same place and then tie the ends together. The few inches of yarn that you lose can be used for ties if you would like. Then tie several pieces of thread around the skein to give the skein extra security. Use a figure-eight knot as in Figure 88.

You are now ready to remove the skein of yarn. On the winder, you will see an obvious place where you can release the tension on the skein and slip the skein free. The niddy noddy will have one arm with a smooth area that allows you to slip the skein free.

With the skeins wound and secured with ties, you are now ready to wet finish and set the twist in your handspun yarn. Congratulations on a job well done!

Figure 87. Wind the yarn on your niddy noddy to make a skein.

Figure 88. Use figure-eight knots in several places to secure your skein.

8

Setting the Twist

After you have wound your plied yarn into a skein and secured it with several ties, it's time to remove the skein from the niddy noddy or skein winder. First of all, take a moment to admire your work. Good for you and congratulations on your beautifully spun yarn! There are many types of yarn. Some are smooth, as if they were spun in a factory, and some are quite textured. You could say that they're a little uneven or a bit rough. "Designer yarn" is what some people call these highly textured skeins. In any case, there is a place for all yarns and a place to use them in your work. Please never compare your yarns to a mill-spun yarn that's spun on an automated machine. There is just no comparison between these two. Your handspun yarn represents your love and time in every inch of that yarn and throughout the whole skein. Cheers!

As you admire your skein of yarn, do you notice any additional twisting in the skein? It's not unusual for this to happen (see Figure 89). Rarely does a skein of yarn hang straight when you hold it straight out in front of you. If your skein twists back on itself, it's simply displaying that it has additional energy. A small amount can be overlooked and will be fine. When the skein of yarn twists back on itself several times, you want to block the yarn to set and release that built-up energy. Why?

If you knit with overenergized yarn, you often see the knitted stitches leaning to one side instead of stacking on top of one another (see Figure 90). Imagine looking at a sweater where the intended vertical cables lean hard to the right or left. It sort of ruins the design, doesn't it?

Fabrics that have been woven with overenergized yarn will sometimes display a characteristic known as tracking. For example, a length of cloth that has

Figure 89. Most freshly spun yarn will have a bit of twist, like this, and you will want to block it to release that built-up energy.

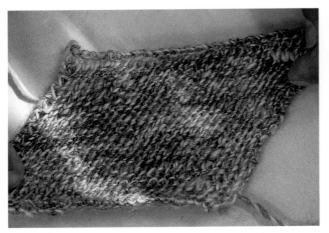

Figure 90. A swatch of knitting with overenergized yarn.

been woven as plain weave will appear to have twill patterning. Unintentional diagonal lines will move across the surface of the fabric. Interesting and sometimes distracting results happen from using these energized threads.

To reduce that energy, a final step known as blocking or setting the twist is necessary. Over the years I have read and tried several different methods for setting twist. What follows the method that I return to again and again. It's simple and fast, and the technique is similar to blanching vegetables.

Start by placing a large pot of water on a stove and heat it to simmering. Next, place a second large pot of cold water on the counter beside the stove and next to the pot of hot water. Slide your skein of yarn into the pot of hot water and watch it relax in the water. It seems to ease the tension in the skein the same as a nice hot bath relaxes you after a stressful day. It only takes a minute in the hot water bath. Then carefully lift the skein out of the hot water with a pair of cooking tongs (see Figure 91). Let some of the water drain out. Now, slide the hot, steaming skein into the pot of cold water. The shock in water temperatures sets the twist, and your overenergized yarn is relaxed and soon ready to use. It only needs to dry.

To dry your skeins of yarn, simply hang them on a drying rack or place them on a dowel rod to drip. You can first squeeze a lot of water out of the yarn by simply using your hands. You can also use a washing machine—spin cycle only—to extract most of the water. A salad spinner also works well. For fun, give your neighbors something to talk about: Hold the wet skeins in your hand and spin the skeins over your head right out there in the lawn. It's guaranteed to start a conversation.

Figure 91. Use tongs to move your skein from hot to cold water.

Figure 92. Energized skein that should be blocked.

For many years, different books have advised spinners to hang their wet skeins outside with a heavy weight on them to block the yarn. As the skeins dry this way under tension, it tends to take the elasticity out of the yarn. That elasticity is cherished by most knitters. This method of blocking yarn works fine for hand-weaving yarns, but for knitting yarn, well, knitters like the springiness left in the yarn. It helps to define the stitch. So if you want to keep your yarns springy, just let them hang naturally to dry.

If you have removed the skein from your winder and you notice that it is perfectly balanced, you need not do anything else before using this beautiful yarn, although I do like to soak my skeins in a sink of warm, soapy water for a few minutes. Simply use a mild, gentle soap such as shampoo or dish soap. A little bit does wonders. Rinse in warm water and hang up to dry as described above.

I can't tell you enough about how wonderful it is to create a garment or another project using your own handspun yarn. I think you are going to be hooked.

CONCLUSION

It is my wish that you come to find spinning as much fun and as enjoyable as I do. I hope you find the information that I have given you here helpful and that it will get you on your way to experiencing many hours of spinning pleasure. As you try new and different fibers, embrace the experience as a new adventure. Some you will like, and some you won't. That's exactly how we find out and decide how we want to spend our precious hours. There is no sense in spending many hundreds of hours spinning a fiber you don't enjoy. Chances are you won't enjoy the hours spent knitting the sweater from that yarn, either. Life is too short!

I have learned to keep an open mind regarding what I think I am going to like and not like. For instance, I told myself that spinning cotton would be a challenge and I most likely wouldn't enjoy it. But I set a goal, telling myself that I only had to spin enough cotton to weave a dish towel. I sometimes set a goal for myself, and once I meet that goal, I move on. I can then say I did it and can put that fiber experience away and forget it. Well, to my amazement, I love spinning cotton. Now I want to try spinning every variety and color. I have even tried growing my own cotton. I totally surprised myself.

In the introduction I asked you, "Why do you want to spin?" I always ask this question of my students. The answers are always interesting and sometimes surprising, though I have never heard someone say, "To save money by spinning my own yarn."

Some students are already raising animals for their fiber. These folks want to have a better understanding of how their fiber contributes to yarn making. Other people are interested in the history of spinning thread. These folks want to demonstrate spinning to the public. It's their mission to show the uninformed just where their clothes and textiles come from. I totally applaud these folks. Some are required to wear period clothing to properly represent a certain time period. Other spinners will go out into the public wearing their modern, comfortable clothes and show that spinning is timeless and happening now. These folks are showing that spinning is not "old timey."

Whatever your reason, and you certainly don't even need a reason, enjoy your spinning. Spinning is relaxing and calming. It's fun to spin by yourself or with a group of friends. A gathering of friends who are like-minded and understand your passion is a good thing. Spouses and family are required to say, "That's nice." Spinners' groups are also a great way to ask questions and get answers from experienced spinners.

Spinning is just like any other skill: it gets better and easier with practice. In the beginning, there is always a sense of frustration and the feeling that this is more difficult than you thought. Hang in there. You're going to get it and then have the time of your life. You might even hear yourself saying, "It can wait—I have another bobbin to spin before I stop."

Happy spinning!

GLOSSARY

Attenuate. To draw out the fibers between your hands and under tension. This can be done with a short draw as if to spin a worsted yarn or can be done as a long draw when spinning for a woolen-spun yarn.

Batt. The carded wool produced on a drum carder.

Bobbin. The spool on which spun yarn is stored. The bobbin is found on the flyer of a spinning wheel.

Carding. The process of taking cleaned and picked fibers and straightening those fibers so they are aligned. This can be done with the use of hand carders or a drum carder. Fine wire teeth that are embedded into carding cloth brush against each other to straighten the fibers. Carding cloth is found on hand carders and drum carders and also mounted on the larger drums of commercial carders.

Cloud. This is a term often used to describe the teased or picked fibers before they are carded.

Combed top. This is a term used to describe a prepared fiber that has the fibers aligned all in the same direction. Commercially prepared combed top is used to spin worsted yarns.

Combing. A fiber preparation that aligns and straightens the fibers so they lie parallel to one another. In the processing, shorter fibers are separated away as waste.

Crimp. This describes the natural wave found in wool fibers. Different breeds of sheep have varying amounts of crimp. Finer wools tend to have more crimp than coarser wool breeds. Crimp helps to aid in the elasticity a yarn has.

Diz. A disk used in the drafting process when removing combed top from combs. It is often concave and can have one hole or multiple holes of different sizes to help regulate the thickness of the combed top. It can be made of beautiful wood or be as simple as a piece of PVC pipe or even a fender washer.

Draft. To draw out or attenuate the fibers just before the twist is entered into the yarn. Drafting can also be done to combed fibers and carded fibers such as a rolag or a batt.

Drum carder. Equipment resembling a small, scaled-down version of a commercial carding mill: a frame with two different-sized drums that are mounted with carding cloth. The smaller drum is known as a "licker in" drum, and the larger drum is the carding drum. When fibers are entered onto the drums, the fibers pass over the teeth of the carding cloth and get straightened. The carded fibers are removed from the drum carder and called a batt.

Flicker. Resembling a small and narrow hand card, a flicker is used to open up the shorn and tip end of a lock of wool. You can spin directly from the teased locks or you can feed them onto the feeding tray of a drum carder.

Flyer. The flyer on a wheel spins to introduce the twist into the thread. It also draws the spun yarn onto the bobbin for storage.

Hand cards. Hand cards resemble a pair of paddles that are covered with carding cloth. The tiny bent-wire teeth in the carding cloth straighten the picked wool. Hand cards are used to make rolags for woolen-spun yarns but can be used for blending fibers or for experimenting with color blends.

Hand combs. Hand combs are used in the preparation of combed top. They are sometimes referred to as Viking combs or English combs. Viking combs usually have one or two rows of long tines and work well to align long-stapled wool. English combs, however, have five rows of tines and work very well on long-stapled wool or shorter-stapled wools. English combs also work well to separate the long fibers from the shorter fibers on dual-coated fleeces. The longer fibers can be drafted off, leaving the shorter fibers remaining in the tines.

Lanolin. The naturally excreted grease from sheep.

Lazy Kate. A rack or frame used to hold filled bobbins when you are plying.

Long draw. This is a spinning technique that is used to make a woolen-spun yarn. While one hand pinches and holds the twist close to the flyer's orifice, the other hand draws the prepared fiber backward to an arm's length. The forward hand releases small amounts of twist to stabilize the yarn. When the spinner is satisfied with the amount of twist in the yarn, the spinner moves the extended arm forward to allow the spun yarn to wind onto the bobbin. Then the process continues again.

Memory. This is a term used to describe the elasticity in a yarn. Yarns spun from fine wools with larger amounts of crimp will have more elasticity, or memory, than yarns spun from coarser breeds of sheep.

Niddy noddy. A niddy noddy is used to make a skein of yarn. There is a center pole and two crossbars that are mounted perpendicularly. Niddy noddies are usually found constructed to measure lengths of 1- to 2-yard skeins. By counting the revolutions, a spinner can get an idea of how many yards there are in a finished skein.

Picking. This term describes pulling the wool locks apart. This is a preliminary step before carding. Teasing or picking fleece helps to remove small particles of vegetal matter.

Ply. The process of twisting two or more single-spun yarns together. Usually, two Z-spun singles are plied together in a counterclockwise direction to make an S-plied yarn. Three- and four-ply yarns are not uncommon.

Rolag. Rolags are created on hand carders for spinning woolen-spun yarns. As a rolag is removed from the carders, it resembles a woolly jelly roll. The fibers lie perpendicular to the length of the rolag. Spinning takes place from the end of the rolag.

Roving. A fiber preparation that is commercially produced on drum carders. The carded fibers lie somewhat parallel to each other and are drawn off the carding machine in a ropelike appearance.

Scour. A washing process that is used to remove impurities from the fleece.

Second cuts. Short lengths of wool found in a shorn fleece. They are the result of the shearer's clippers going back over an area that has already been clipped. These second cuts are too short to spin by themselves and are the cause of irregularities in the yarn.

Skein. A continuous length of yarn that is made into a loop. With secure ties added throughout the skein, it can be tightly twisted to make an attractive package.

Skirting. This is the process of removing undesirable portions of a fleece. Often the neck, belly, and leg wool are removed from the shorn fleece. This is also a good time to remove all manure tags and second cuts.

Staple. A length of fleece also known as a lock.

Suint. This is sheep sweat and sometime leaves yellow stains in a fleece.

Vegetal matter (VM). Sheep that are not coated will pick up hay, straw, burrs, and weed seeds. VM is definitely not something you want in your fleece and spun yarn.

Whorl. The whorl on a spinning wheel flyer is the pulley that determines the ratio speeds between the drive wheel and the flyer. A whorl can also be found on a hand spindle.

Woolen. This is a term used to describe both a fiber preparation and a style of spinning.

Worsted. Just like the term "woolen," this term describes a fiber preparation and a technique of spinning. It is also used to describe a weight or size of a yarn.

Yolk. This is the yellow stain found in a fleece, and it doesn't wash away during scouring.

FURTHER READING

Amos, Alden. *The Alden Amos Big Book of Handspinning.* New York: Interweave Press, 2001.

Anderson, Sarah. *The Spinner's Book of Yarn Designs: Techniques for Creating 80 Yarns.* North Adams, MA: Storey Publishing, 2013.

Blacker, Susan. *Pure Wool: A Guide to Using Single-Breed Yarn.* Guilford, CT: Stackpole, 2012.

Callahan, Gail. *Hand Dyeing Yarn and Fleece: Dip-Dyeing, Hand-Painting, Tie-Dyeing, and Other Creative Techniques.* North Adams, MA: Storey Publishing, 2010.

Casey, Maggie. *Start Spinning: Everything You Need to Know to Make Great Yarn.* New York: Interweave Press, 2008.

Field, Anne. *Spinning Wool: Beyond the Basics.* North Pomfret, VT: Trafalgar Square Books, 2010.

Fournier, Nola, and Jane Fournier. *In Sheep's Clothing: A Handspinner's Guide to Wool.* New York: Interweave Press, 1995.

Franquemont, Abby. *Respect the Spindle.* New York: Interweave Press, 2009.

Larson, Kate. *The Practical Spinner's Guide—Wool.* New York: Interweave Press, 2015.

Lo, Felicia. *Dyeing to Spin & Knit: Techniques & Tips to Make Custom Hand-Dyed Yarns.* New York: Interweave, 2017.

Martineau, Ashley. *Spinning and Dyeing Yarn: The Home Spinner's Guide to Creating Traditional and Art Yarns.* New York: B.E.S. Publishing, 2013.

Moreno, Jillian. *Yarnitecture: A Knitter's Guide to Spinning: Building Exactly the Yarn You Want.* North Adams, MA: Storey Publishing, 2016.

Robson, Deborah, and Carol Ekarius. *The Fleece & Fiber Sourcebook: More than 200 Fibers from Animal to Spun Yarn.* North Adams, MA: Storey Publishing, 2011.

Smith, Beth. *The Spinner's Book of Fleece: A Breed-by-Breed Guide to Choosing and Spinning the Perfect Fiber for Every Purpose.* North Adams, MA: Storey Publishing, 2014.

Stove, Margaret. *Merino: Handspinning, Dyeing, and Working with Merino and Superfine Wool.* New York: Interweave Press, 1991.

ACKNOWLEDGMENTS

Thank you, Candi Derr, my editor, for encouraging me to write this book. It's always a pleasure to work with you on a new project. To Kathy Eckhaus, my talented photographer, thank you for capturing the right shot to help better explain what I was trying to say through text. You folks are the BEST!

I would also like to thank my daughter, Sara Bixler, and her husband, Dustin, for allowing us to use their beautiful studio (Red Stone Glen Fiber Arts Studio) and property for the photos in this book. Thank you.

Buses In Colour - Volume Two

IN AND AROUND HUDD

Robert Berry

HUDDERSFIELD

36

VIA NEW MILL

23

ACX 323A

Nostalgia Road Publications

CONTENTS:

Front Cover: *Trolleybus 629 was one of the several 1956 BUT 9641T models in the Huddersfield fleet.* Strathwood Library.

Rear Cover Bottom: *One of Baddeley Brother's Bedford VAM models with Plaxton bodywork sits in the sun at Huddersfield.* H. J. Black

Rear Cover Top: *One of the two of AEC Reliances new to Hanson in 1967.* H. J. Black

Title Page: *A Roe-bodied AEC Reliance rests in Huddersfield bus station.* H. J Black

This Page: *A 1966 Hanson Reliance.* Strathwood Library

The **Buses in Colour** Series™

is produced under licence by

Nostalgia Road Publications Ltd.
Units 5-8, Chancel Place, Shap Road Industrial Estate,
Kendal, Cumbria, LA9 6NZ
Tel.+44 (0)1539 738832 - Fax: +44 (0)1539 730075

designed and published by
Trans-Pennine Publishing Ltd.
PO Box 10, Appleby-in-Westmorland, Cumbria, CA16 6FA
Tel.+44 (0)17683 51053 Fax.+44 (0)17683 53558
e-mail:admin@transpenninepublishing.co.uk

and printed by
Kent Valley Colour Printers Ltd.
Kendal, Cumbria +44 (0)1539 741344

INTRODUCTION

The town of Huddersfield, in the West Riding of Yorkshire, is without doubt one of the largest in the country, and should (many say) be given city status. It is a town of many facets ranging from the remnants of grim industrialisation to stunning surrounding countryside. At its central core is proud Victorian architecture, and evidence of the high level of prosperity that was founded on its primary industries of textiles, engineering and chemicals.

The town, and the surrounding area have long been served by a fascinating array of public service vehicles, by fleets from both within the town and outlying areas. The need for transporting high volumes of the passengers was of course due to the fact that the area became one of the most prominent textile-manufacturing towns in the north of England during the industrial revolution.

Above: *Huddersfield bus 128 was one of a group of six 1969 Roe-bodied Daimler Fleetlines (RCX 128G). This was actually the very last vehicle taken into the JOC fleet, however it is viewed shortly after the merger of the two fleets, after being re-painted in the combined livery* Strathwood Library

Huddersfield also became the home of such famous names as Karrier Motors, Imperial Chemical Industries (previously British Dyes), L. B. Holiday (chemicals), Hopkinson's Valves, Brook Electric Motors, Harold H. Haigh, Holset Engineering, Mitre Sports, Ben Shaws (mineral waters), and of course the David Brown plants; David Brown Gears at Lockwood and St. Andrew's Road, and the massive David Brown Tractors works at Meltham. Huddersfield also gained renowned fame thanks to its worsted industry, which was turned into high quality men's suits the world over.

But along with industrialisation came the grime of industrial life, and many people will recall a time when skies were heavy with the steady noxious waste of innumerable mill chimneys towering into the heavens. Most of these mills saw a mass exodus of the working class at the end of their shift, so transport (trains, trams and buses) were all needed in large numbers. Yet, as all Yorkshiremen know, 'where there's muck there's brass' and Huddersfield once had more Rolls Royce and Bentley cars than any other town in Britain. Only a few merchants and mill owners could aspire to such status symbols, but their employees could stare through the windows of the elite local dealership and body-builder (Rippon Brothers) in Viaduct Street, and dream!

Industrialisation was the town's *raison-detre*, but it also confused its boundaries, as there was an almost continuous link with the neighbouring towns of Elland, Halifax, Brighouse, Cleckheaton, Mirfield and Dewsbury. By contrast, the areas around Flockton in the east, Marsden in the west, and the market town of Holmfirth in the south were truly rural. These areas also served to support the industrial communities, for here were the principal farming areas supplying dairy, agricultural and horticultural produce to Huddersfield and the smaller market towns of this part of the West Riding.

Below: *During the long years of service to the town and the surrounding area, Huddersfield buses were based at two depots. This is the Longroyd Bridge garage. The thoroughfare to the right of the picture is St. Thomas Road along which was the original Karrier Works, where many of Huddersfield's trolleybus chassis were built.*
Strathwood Collection

To the south and south-east of this fertile area was the northern perimeter of South Yorkshires coalfield, with its related contribution to employment for the people of this district, and in consequence also provided the most common supply of fuel at this time.

With the coming of the Industrial Revolution, there came also the need for a more practical and efficient method of transporting the public. Enterprising farmers, carters and carriers recognised the potential of this by the adoption of a horse-drawn waggon, fitted with removable seats to transport workers or people to market for a small fee.

Above: *This is No.535 (BVH 135), which was painted in a red, white and blue livery with suitable embellishments to celebrate the coronation of HRH Queen Elizabeth II in 1953.*
East Lanc/Huddersfield Corporation official.

This proved so successful that some of these businesses had special horse-drawn bus bodies built, later progressing to motorbuses. This was the basis for many of the independent local public service companies that flourished, not only in the area under discussion, but also throughout the length and breadth of the British Isles.

By the 1860s, public transport in Huddersfield and the surrounding area was provided by several people operating horse-drawn buses. Such services became even more important as the growing town became a Municipal Borough in 1868. In the mid-19th century Huddersfield was provided with a magnificent railway station, the foundation stone being laid by Earl Fitzwilliam on 9th October 1846. The poet, John Betjeman later praised the station's architectural beauty, which had a frontage with a central projecting portico of eight Corinthian columns. Even now it is one of the most elegant of its kind in Britain, as are the buildings of the 'new town' that was extended eastward from the Market Place to join up with it.

Huddersfield's dream of its own transport system was realised in 1883, when the town became the first municipality to build and operate its own steam tramway system. The first route to be opened was from Lockwood (Red Lion Hotel), to Fartown (Royal Hotel) on the 11th January 1883.

The Huddersfield Tramways Committee was appointed at a council meeting on 9th November 1885 and its first meeting was held the following day. Prior to this there had been a Tramways Sub-Committee, which had looked at the proposals to build a tramway system. From 8th June 1936 it was known as the Passenger Transport Committee and its last meeting took place on 11th March 1974. By the end of the century 19 different steam-tram routes were operated. However, the six original Wilkinson tram engines were soon sold in part exchange for larger engines, as these were needed to cater for the increased volume of passenger traffic.

Work was started on electrifying the network in 1899, and by 1902 the system was completely electrified and extended beyond the Borough boundary. The Corporation Tramway Department soon found competition for this lucrative business from many small bus operators that were already established locally! Given the steps that the Corporation used to protect its interests, some of these operators faced a Sisyphean task and were to succumb to financial problems. Other enterprises maintained a large-degree of fortitude and became very well respected as well as patronised.

In this volume we will take a look at the major, and some of the minor, bus and coach operators that have served the population of one of Britain's largest towns during the first century of public service vehicles.

Above: *The entire fleet of Huddersfield trolleybuses were all of this tri-axle design, although built by various chassis manufacturers. Sunbeam S7, PVH 931 was among the last batch of this design of trolleybuses to be supplied to a British trolleybus system.* Strathwood Library

The majority of these are no longer in existence, and many of their garages have been razed to the ground. Inevitably, the book that follows is very clearly a personal trip down Nostalgia Road, I make no apologies for this, for this is the essence of these publications by Trans-Pennine to recall a former way of life and recapture an era that is now but a fading memory.

Robert Berry   Penrith, October 2005

HUDDERSFIELD CORPORATION

As mentioned in the introduction, Huddersfield had the proud distinction of operating the very first British municipal passenger transport service. This pioneering venture, when started in 1883, utilised the operation of steam tram engines towing double-deck passenger cars. However, when the route to Moldgreen was inaugurated in 1885, it used horse-drawn trams for the first three years. This was because the King Street section was considered unsuitable for steam trams at this time, and the problem wasn't adequately resolved until the entire system was completely electrified. Rather than incur the considerable expense of extending the system over routes that

Above: *Here we see big (KVH 219) a 1956 BUT 9641T, with East Lancs bodywork. It is working on the cross-town Route 71 from Waterloo to Lindley, as is sister vehicle KVH 222, seen working in the opposite direction. The Huddersfield-Lindley portion of the working was used regularly by my family and I.* H. John Black

would prove to be less lucrative, the Transport Department obtained powers under the Transport Act in 1913 to operate motorbuses; the basic idea behind this was for the motorbuses to act as a feeder service to the tramway system.

With the outbreak of World War I in 1914; the motorbus option was not immediately integrated into the transport system. However, with a return to peace it was considered prudent to extend the transport system once more. Accordingly, the Huddersfield firm of Karrier Motors was approached, and this resulted in the purchase of two Karrier K4 chassis; the first one was a 30-seat single-deck bus bodied by the General Seating Company.

This was given fleet number 2, and registered CX 4267, whilst the second one, an open-top double-deck bus (registered CX 4268) was given the fleet number 4. Numbers 1 and 3 are believed to have been numbers allocated to tramway maintenance vehicles at this time. These buses were painted in the same livery as the trams; a splendid deep maroon colour on the lower panels with the window surrounds and upper bodywork a pale ivory cream colour. The local crest and the name Huddersfield Corporation Tramways adorned the lower panels of the buses, and (like the trams) the paintwork was traditionally lined out.

On the motorbuses' first journey of the morning, passengers could ride the whole way from the town centre to the ultimate destination of Golcar (Town End), and also again on the last run of the day, when the bus was to return to the depot..

Top Right: *When Huddersfield Corporation decided to withdraw their trolleybus system in favour of motorbuses, the initial choice was two batches of these Leyland Titans. Of these, UCX 407 was the penultimate member of the first order for Roe-bodied PD3A/2s.* H. John Black

Bottom Right: *Succeeding the Leyland Titans of 1961/2, Daimler found favour. Following ten Roe-bodied CVG6LX/30 models, came six East Lancs-bodied examples, these were also delivered in 1964. Here CCX 439B wears an almost identical version of the streamlined Corporation livery to that used on the Leylands.* H. John Black.

In between these times, the bus was used as a shuttle service from Golcar to the tramway terminus at Paddock Head. The motorbuses proved so successful that further routes were added, resulting in the need for further buses. By the end of the following year, six motorbuses were in stock. This figure was made up from three more single-deck buses and a new open-top double-deck bus; all of which were based on the Karrier K4 chassis.

During 1924, the Tramways Department was experiencing competition from private bus companies who were running 'through services' to the town centre. Quite understandably, from a passenger's point of view, it made more sense to ride through to the town centre on one bus rather than switch to a tram to complete the journey. To overcome this challenge from 22nd March 1924, the Meltham to Lockwood and the Kirkheaton to Moldgreen routes were extended to run through to the town centre as motorbus routes. These then competed with

Baddeley Brothers on their Meltham route and also with another local firm, County Motors, who ran through Kirkheaton on their Dewsbury service. New vehicles continued to be added to the fleet, not only to allow for route extension but also to replace time-served vehicles too. During 1927 Huddersfield even purchased one of the rare three-axle Karrier WL6/1 models, which was bodied by Northern Counties as a dual-door 36-seat single-deck bus and given the fleet number 60 (VH 1097); it remained in the fleet until 1933, but was the only such example.

During 1931, the Transport Committee were faced with the problem that most of the tramway rolling stock, overhead equipment and track was approaching the end of its useful life. This was especially apparent on the Almondbury route, where early renewal of the track was considered a priority. The renewal costs seemed prohibitive and this therefore gave an opportunity to consider an experiment with trolleybuses; a system that had proved very successful in nearby Bradford.

Left: *During 1969, Huddersfield Corporation Passenger Transport Department took over the Huddersfield JOC fleet and also the routes and stage vehicle fleet of the independent concern, Hanson buses. Waiting in Lindley is Huddersfield 90, a 1965 Roe-bodied AEC Reliance that had previously been 390 in the Hanson fleet.* H. John Black

Below: *Huddersfield Corporation had switched their single-deck allegiance to Seddon during 1970 and remained faithful to this company for the provision of five batches of their RU model. With this new type of chassis there came a new bodybuilder to Huddersfield, for all of these RU models were bodied by Pennine Coachcraft. Showing the new face of Huddersfield buses is CCX 850K.* H. John Black

To facilitate the experiment, a temporary motorbus service was operated via Almondbury (Old Bank) after the last tram to Almondbury ran on 5th December 1932. Meanwhile, Somerset Road was closed to traffic so that the track could be removed and the road resurfaced.

Rather than commit themselves to an initial purchase order, the Committee chose to use six double-deck trolley buses from four different makers of six-wheel chassis, (three Karrier's, and one each from Ransomes, Sunbeam and AEC). These were fitted with various bodies and equipment for the initial experiment, in order to obtain data as to which type of vehicle would be most suitable to a new trolleybus system. The Ransomes, Sims & Jefferies chassis (VH 5723) was the first and it was bodied by Brush.

The results of the trials were encouraging and so 24 Karrier chassis with both English Electric and Metro-Vick electrical equipment were purchased. Indeed as a result of the successful working on the Almondbury and Lindley routes, it was decided to convert the other tram routes to the trolleybus operation. Therefore, from 1937 the tramway system was gradually phased out, with the last Huddersfield tram running on the Brighouse route on 29th June 1940.

Along with the disappearance of the trams, went the traditional Huddersfield livery. Initially the trolleybuses sported a colour scheme using deep maroon on the lower panels, with upper panels painted Post Office red. Three rich cream, bands (almost a lemon colour) were incorporated into this scheme, below the lower and upper-deck windows and between decks.

Later the lower deck band swept around the leading edge of the front mud-guards giving the front of the vehicles an apron of this colour, to distinguish them from the motor buses of the Huddersfield Joint Omnibus Committee (JOC) fleet, which also adopted a similar scheme. Mudguards on these tri-axle buses were black, and so too were the wheels. Later, in the post-war years, the lower deck panels and wheels were also painted in Post Office red, on both the Corporation and the JOC fleets. The Corporation had started using this scheme as early as 1941 on some of their trolleybuses, while during the war years some of the JOC buses had been painted in a grey livery. Karrier E6 three-axle trolley-buses continued to be purchased in large numbers until 1940, after which no more trolleybuses were obtained until 1947.

After the war, Karrier MS2s with Metro-Vick equipment were purchased, these originally had 70-seat bodies by Park Royal but were re-bodied by East Lancashire in 1961. More of these chassis arrived in 1949, but following reorganisation within the Rootes Group these were designated as Sunbeam MS2 models. These examples were bodied by Charles H. Roe of Crossgates, Leeds, where my father had served his apprenticeship. A change of purchasing policy saw the arrival of BUT 9641T chassis, with English-Electric equipment in 1953. Further examples were taken into the fleet in 1956, all with East Lancs H40/32R bodies. The year 1959 saw a return to the Sunbeam chassis, now the S7 model, but these were to be the last six-wheel trolleybus chassis delivered to an English trolleybus system.

The people of Huddersfield were almost unanimous in their love affair with the trolleybus, none more so than my younger brother Michael and I. At the time we lived near the trolleybus terminus Route 20 at Riddings (to Newsome South). Not that I liked the area, but being close to the terminus we nearly always acquired our coveted seat, front off-side, top deck. From here my brother, barely being able to peer over the bottom of the window, would (in his imagination) drive us into town. We would then take another trolleybus on the 71 route to Lindley, or catch one of the re-built AEC Regal's with full-front Roe bodywork (affectionately know as Flying Tanks), on the Hanson route to Weatherhill and our grandparents house on Cowrakes Road.

Top Right: *Hanson's last new vehicles were of these handsome 53-seat Willowbrook-bodied AEC Reliance buses; LCX 34 E was the first of the pair of 1967 models.* H. John Black

Bottom Right: *Pausing on Wakefield Road is (NCX 689) the last numerically of the eight ex-JOC 1958 AEC Regent V models. All but one of these (185) later passed to the WYPTE.* H. John Black

Above: *Fleet 129 defiantly turns its back on the encroaching Civic Centre, which along with the new ring road would erase all traces of the Upperhead bus station within a short time. Registered UCX 129H, it was the first of the 1970 Fleetlines.* H. John Black

Trolleybus networks in the United Kingdom numbered around 50, over 40 of which were municipal systems, and of these, London operated the largest trolleybus network of all. As mentioned earlier, when the cost of maintaining this kind of transport system began increasing and manufacturers were on the decline, a decision was taken to replace the trolleybus network in Huddersfield with motorbuses.

This was indeed sad news and even the local newspaper, *The Huddersfield Examiner* remained pro-trolleybus to the very end. The truth is that trolleybuses were very dear to the heart of local people, and hundreds of people turned out onto the streets to watch their passing on that last day of operation on 13th July 1968.

With the introduction of motorbuses on former trolleybus routes, it became possible to revise the routes to serve a greater area. As motorbuses were not confined to following the overhead network, this often increased revenue from the area served, thus increasing profitability. The first examples of motorbuses purchased as trolleybus replacement vehicles were eight Leyland Titan PD3A/2 half-cab buses with a front entrance. Numbered 401-8, these were bodied by Charles H. Roe and registered UCX 401-8. They were painted in the same livery style as the Corporation-owned trolleybus fleet with their primrose cream aprons, a styling feature that was also repeated on the top deck. Meanwhile the JOC-owned buses were still painted in an overall red livery with three conventional straight bands around the vehicle.

Further examples of the Roe-bodied PD3As were purchased in 1962-3, and given the registrations WVH 409-24; these along with the earlier models had the St. Helens-style fibreglass front. Also in 1962, two of the 11-strong batch of JOC Park Royal-bodied AEC Regent IIIs (DCX 951/5) that had been purchased new in 1947, were transferred to the Corporation fleet and re-painted into the appropriate streamlined livery style. For new buses during the rest of the 1960s, Daimler found favour with two batches of their CVG6LX being delivered in 1964, using bodies by both Roe and East Lancs. More were purchased in 1965, then more East Lancs bodied buses, 457-72 (HVH 457-72D) arrived in 1966. From 1967 onwards, as with other operators, the Daimler Fleetline was purchased in large numbers, primarily for one-man-operation

The Corporation's first examples of the Fleetline CRG6LX models with Gardner engines, arrived in 1967. These were registered KVH 473–88E, and like the second batch deliveries, (OCX 489–504F), they were bodied by Roe. They had a front-entrance and seating for 75 passengers, as did the later batches of CRG6LX models, 129-34 (UCX 129-34H) in 1970, 135-40 (YVH 535-40K) in 1971. Then came ten more chassis 141-50 (GVH141-50L) in 1972, but these last three batches had the new style of Roe bodywork, with seating for 45 in the top deck and 29 in the lower saloon, plus a dual-door configuration.

As stated on page 11, Huddersfield switched to the Seddon Pennine RU for its single-deck fleet from 1970 onwards. However, although Huddersfield was the biggest municipal operator of dual door RUs, the bodies were prone to numerous failures.

Top Right: *John William Street, is the location of the first of the former JOC Leyland Titan PD2A/24s as it pauses before continuing on its journey to Wilberlee.*
H. John Black

Bottom Right: *Originally the Fleetline's of the early 1970s were of dual door layout. but they were later converted to front entrance.*
Strathwood Library

THE HUDDERSFIELD JOINT OMNIBUS COMMITTEE

With the introduction of the 'Road Traffic Act' in 1930, which allowed the railway companies to take an interest in road transport, the Corporation came to an agreement with the LMS Railway. By this 'agreement' the railway company purchased 50% of the motorbus section of the Tramways Department, and together the two undertakings formed the Huddersfield Joint Omnibus Committee (JOC). This arrangement would leave the tramway system totally Corporation-owned, as the JOC came into effect on 16th May 1930. Curiously this system of joint-operation seems to have been a Yorkshire phenomenon, for although several municipal transport departments were approached, only the municipalities of Halifax, Huddersfield, Sheffield, and the small town of Todmorden formed this kind of an alliance.

Above: *Vehicles of Guy Motors manufacture were not very common in the Huddersfield fleet, but a pair of Arab MKIVs and examples of the UF models were used by the JOC.* H. John Black

With the formation of the JOC, minimal alterations were required to show changes to the legal ownership whilst the Corporation crest was replaced. This involved a circular design whereby one half was the Corporation coat-of-arms, while the other side had the railway motif; the wording below reading Huddersfield Corporation & LMS Joint Services in gold lettering. Purchasing policy for the fleet in the main favoured AEC Regent double-deck buses and Regal saloons in the 1930s, although a pair of Leyland Cub single-deckers were bought in 1934. These had bodies by Roe, but a further pair of these 20-seat buses with Roberts bodywork arrived in 1935

During these early years, the JOC bought out a number of privately-owned motorbus services, the most important of these being the acquisition of the 14 -strong vehicle fleet of Wilson Haigh from Holmfirth in June 1934. This company operated several excursions, and had two fare stage services, Holmfirth-Meltham-Marsden on an hourly service, and a 30-minute Huddersfield to Honley service.

During World War II, production of PSVs was suspended by the government, but the shortage of buses therefore became critical, and so the Ministry of Supply allowed Guy Motors to resume production of double-deck chassis. Bedford was also allowed to resume the manufacture of single-deck chassis. These two models were all that was available until 1943, when Daimler were also allowed to recommence the production of a double-deck chassis, also to specified utility standards. Twenty of these Utility double-deck Daimler CWA6s with AEC engines were purchased by the JOC during the last two years of the war and bodied by both Duple and Brush. Of these, CCX 648, the first of the 1944-deliveries, was the only one to have a high-bridge body; the other 19 all being L27/28R models.

All of these Daimlers carried registration numbers in the CCX- sequence, they were CCX 649, 650/1, 660-3, 698-700, 733-7, whilst the last ones, (fleet numbers 216-9), were registered CCX 776-9. These were the last motor buses bought until 1947, when once more AEC chassis were available. However Daimler single-deck buses were purchased between 1948 and 1950.

Top Right: *Huddersfield acquired 20 of the utility Daimler CWA6 models, all but one were low-bridge models. This one, CCX 777 former JOC 217 was one of the 1945 models.* Robert Berry

Bottom Right: *After withdrawal from the JOC fleet during 1955 buses 217 and 219 served for a long time with West Bridgeford UDC.* Strathwood Library.

Top Left: *JOC Bus 173 (FVH 173) was one of a new batch of these highbridge double-deckers that entered service in October 1951. The batch consisted of buses with fleet numbers 170-5. These AEC Regent IIIs were the first eight-feet-wide buses in the fleet.* H. John Black

Bottom Left: *A comparison with the above photograph, is this study of one of the many buses built to low-bridge specification in the Huddersfield JOC fleet. Particular notice will be given to the squarer roof profile, the four-abreast seating and off-side sunken gangway. Bus number 233 was a 1954 AEC Regent III, again like the vehicle above, it was furnished with East Lancs bodywork and was the second of eight identical vehicles (HVH 232-9), all of which were withdrawn between 1971 and 1972.* H. John Black

The year 1952 saw the surprise purchase of two Guy Arab UF, under floor engine 43-seat buses (FVH 1-2). These had their ranks swelled when five more were added to the fleet in 1954, numbers 3-7 (GVH 793-7). All seven of these were bodied by Guy/Park Royal. Incidentally these buses were the first JOC buses to feature Huddersfield prominently as a fleet-name on the front panel below the windscreen (as seen on page 16). The livery of these buses was in keeping with the fleet, being an overall post office red with a narrow cream band around the bus. On withdrawal, the two earlier buses found their way into the Stockport Social Services fleet, while some of the later examples served for a time in the fleet of Green Bus of Rugeley in Staffordshire.

During the time up to the 1960s, there were no external advertisements on either the Corporation or the JOC buses, presumably because this sort of thing was deemed unsightly. However, from the late-1940s, advertisements were featured inside the lower deck of the double-deck buses on the cant rails above the side windows.

These were all to a standard size of 16-inches wide by 6-inches deep, but the content and style of these advertisements had to meet the General Manager's approval! A few of the JOC double-deck buses even had a convex, Perspex screen mounted above the lower-deck bulkhead windows with revolving advertisements. One I remember clearly was for Streamline Taxis, it simply illustrated a car and quoted the telephone number 23426, adding 'Remember, 23 for 2/6d'.

Because of some of the structures on their routes, a percentage of the JOC fleet double-deck buses were of 'low-bridge' design. Consequently the AEC Regents, like the war-time Daimler CWA models, had the traditional sunken side gangway on the upper deck. In the main the JOC tended to work the rural or longer routes, including joint services like Route 38 (Huddersfield-Brighouse-Bradford) with Hebble and Bradford Corporation.

Above: *As replacements for some of the ageing Brush-bodied AEC Regents that were withdrawn during the late 1940s, Huddersfield JOC purchased half a dozen of these Regent III models with NCB. bodywork. Former bus 225 (ECX 420-5) was numerically the last of these, but when withdrawn it continued to serve as a driver training bus.* H. John Black

Meanwhile Halifax JOC shared Route 43 with Huddersfield JOC, through Elland and West Vale. The JOC also served on what had been the original tram-feeder routes, operating on some three dozen or so routes, and having some joint workings with Hanson's buses. Another important date to bear in mind in this period was 1st January 1948, when the LMS Railway was nationalised and vested into British Railways, so livery and legal lettering changes took place on the fleet as soon as possible thereafter.

Top Left: *Picking up passengers in the town centre of Huddersfield on the Cowcliffe route is JOC 20. This 1960 Reliance along with sister vehicle SCX 19, would continue to serve Huddersfield through to the formation of the WYPTE. Each then had their fleet number preceded by the figure 40, before receiving the new livery.* H. John Black

Bottom Left: *Making a brief sojourn into the former Upperhead bus station, on a warm summer day is GVH 979, one of the five, 1954 Guy Arab UF models. Next to it is LVH 12 a 1956 Roe-bodied AEC Reliance. Both buses proudly display the Huddersfield JOC. fleetname.* H. John Black

Drivers and conductors working on both the Corporation and the JOC buses were issued with dark blue uniforms, although lightweight jackets of a buff colour were issued for summer-wear. At the time that I was at school, I believe that the conductors used Ultimate ticket machines. I can recall vividly the conductor walking down the aisle of the bus with a heavy looking dark brown satchel on his right hip and the barrel like, chrome ticket machine on his left. Even as a child, if an inspector got on wearing his navy blue overcoat and official peaked hat, I felt a sense of foreboding.

New vehicle buying policy of the JOC in the 1950s and '60s reflected that of many Yorkshire municipal fleets with AEC Regent IIIs being favoured for the double-deck buses. Yet as there was a need for a certain number of single-deck buses too, the orders for these also went in the main to AEC for their Reliance chassis. But it was not always the case and during 1949-50 a handful of Daimler CVG6 Willowbrook-bodied single-deck buses had been bought and these remained in the fleet for a decade. In each of the years 1958 and 1960 the purchase of several exposed-radiator AEC Regent V double-deck buses was noted, whilst a smart pair of East Lancs-bodied Guy Arab IV buses arrived in 1959.

This body-builder also supplied a pair of concealed radiator Regent Vs in 1961, 194-5 (SCX 194-5). These were followed by half a dozen very similar models that were bodied by Roe, 196-201 (UVH 196-201) in 1962. Leyland Titan PD2A/24s, 101-6 (XCX 101-6), also arrived in 1962. These were similar in appearance to the Corporation PD3As of 1961, but used the shorter chassis, which gave seating for 65 passengers. During 1964 and 1965 there followed four batches of Roe-bodied Daimlers, both CVG6LX and CVG6LX/30 models.

The Huddersfield JOC catered for a crucial need, as they served very rural and isolated locations, like the moorland public house of Nont's Sarahs or Wood Nook above Honley.

Some of the smaller hamlets had been campaigning for a bus service for a number of years without success. Several Kirkheaton councillors took up the gauntlet on behalf of the 'forgotten village', the small hamlet of Houses Hill. For, although the JOC had agreed in principle to run a service as far back as 1935, it was not until the Meltham Branch railway was closed in 1949 to passenger traffic, and the JOC. were confident of extra profits from this route that they were encouraged to finally start a new route to Houses Hill. This new service commenced on 22nd May 1949, as Route 15. This started in Huddersfield town centre on Byram Street, and followed the Kirkheaton route. The first bus to operate there was one of the utility Daimler CWA6, 205 (CCX 661), and this made news in the local newspaper.

Top Right: *Huddersfield JOC acquired eight of these very handsome AEC Regent V 2D2RA models, (SCX 194-5) with East Lancs bodies. They entered the fleet in 1960 and two years later 196-201 (UVH 196-201) arrived.* H. John Black

Bottom Right: *Huddersfield had joint working on Route 64 with Bradford City. Bus 114, was one of four Daimler CVG6LX/30s that were new in 1964.* H. John Black.

Above: *Favourite bodybuilders for the two Huddersfield fleets for saloons and double-deck buses had for decades been Roe and East Lancs. Others were tried, particularly in the later years, as bus 26 illustrates. It (KVH 26E) was one of a pair of Leyland PSU4/2R with Neepsend bodies although in reality Neepsend was a part of East Lancs.* H. John Black

The 1967 and 1968 intake was three pairs of saloons on the following chassis, Leyland PSU4 (KVH 25-6E), AEC Swift with Roe bodies (MVH 27-8F), and Daimler CRG6LX also bodied by Roe (PCX 29-30G). The following year, witnessed the arrival of six of the Daimler CRG6LX double-deck buses, which were given the fleet numbers 123-8 (RCX 123-8G).

These were bodied by Charles Roe, and were very similar to the examples that were taken into stock by the Corporation. but they were of course painted in the traditional Huddersfield JOC livery. These were the final buses ordered by the JOC as it passed into Huddersfield Corporation ownership on 1st October 1969, as all British Railway's road transport holdings were divested following the 1968 Transport Act.

The end of the decade affected the whole of the British bus travelling public, for this was the era that marked the start of the National Bus Company. Many Passenger Transport Executives were set up all over Britain to oversee the running of what had been over a very large number of municipal-owned bus fleets. These were merged into large local regions with the once-proud and very individual undertakings (and their traditional liveries),

giving way to a uniform and often nondescript modern identity. Huddersfield was to become Metro-Kirklees, whilst Halifax merged with Todmorden to form Metro-Calderdale. Together along with Bradford and Leeds they were all to form the West Yorkshire Passenger Transport Executive, all of whom had previously employed traditional, well-loved liveries in the areas they served.

Below: *For some unaccountable reason bus 125 (RCX 125G), one of the very last of the JOC buses, is standing outside the Princess Cinema in Northumberland Street facing the wrong way displaying Route 78, the Taylor Hill service. The vending machines dispensed cigarettes, chocolate bars and hot drinks.* H. John Black

CHANGING TIMES

After the absorption of the JOC fleet by Huddersfield Corporation, experiments were put in hand to find a new livery for the integrated fleets; this exercise displayed some rather radical and startling versions of the traditional red and cream livery for a while. Leyland Titan 419 (WVH 419), and one of the 1965 Daimler CVG6LXs, 118 (EVH 118 C), wore an overall red livery with no cream relief whatsoever on the back or sides, although the entire front was painted cream below the roof dome, giving them quite an eerie aspect especially in the dark.

The second experimental livery involved one of the 1958 exposed-radiator Regent Vs with Roe bodywork, (NCX 688), which was painted in an overall red scheme. Once again the front of the bus was painted cream, but this time only up to the

Above: *Former JOC 102,(XCX 102) was one of the six 1963 Leyland Titan PD2A/24s and one of the three buses to be painted into the first of the experimental liveries. Although utilising the same colours, after years of the traditional application of the Corporation and JOC fleets, this scheme not only looked radical but quite eerie on a dark morning.* H. John Black

base of the upper deck window. Cream also was applied to the sides of this bus, but just around the lower deck windows and the area immediately above to the midway beading. The application of the colour scheme in this way seemed to find favour, as this livery was ultimately decided upon, although the panel below the driver's windscreen was painted red instead of cream.

Top Right: *Not the best of photographs, but it is included for its great interest. With the new law courts and a Hanson AEC Regal in the background, we see NCX 688, a 1958 AEC Regent V. Along with two of the 1963 Leyland Titan's, 188 was chosen to model the second style of experimental livery to gauge the public's reaction.* Strathwood Library

Bottom Right: *The second experimental livery, was very close to the application of the colour scheme that was finally chosen for the combined fleets. As 461 shows, the difference being confined to the colour of the front apron.* H. John Black

The merger of the two fleets was to prove to be a short-lived venture, as local government reorganisation of the early-1970s would result in the setting up of a Passenger Transport Executive Board for the day-to-day operation of buses in Huddersfield, Halifax, Leeds, and Bradford. This situation brought about the transfer of certain vehicles with Huddersfield acquiring some Leeds Daimler CVG6LXs, whilst Bradford were supplied with the AEC Regents of Huddersfield.

This was a logical step as it pooled buses of a certain manufacture to certain depots, along with a centralisation of spares etc. At first it was intended that each of the former municipal undertakings would retain a certain individual, although corporate livery, their having a shared buttermilk colour scheme, but retaining a relief colour appropriate to its own former colours. To this end (in December 1973) one of the 1967 Huddersfield Fleetlines, 487 (KVH 48-7E), was painted a buttermilk and red scheme and given the fleet name Metro Kirklees. This was to be the standard application of livery with Leeds retaining a shade of green for its relief colour, Bradford blue and Halifax orange. Along with my editor, Alan Earnshaw, and Mike Goddard from the undertaking, we took this newly-painted bus on its first public appearance around Huddersfield.

Top Left: *The original WYPTE livery had stripes around the cab incorporated into the first version of the livery, but this was soon simplified. This bus, 4121, was originally one of six Daimler CVG6LX/30 (EVH 117-22C) that were new to the JOC in 1965.*
Robert Berry Collection

Bottom Left: *Huddersfield Corporation's first batch of Daimler Fleetline models (473-88), were delivered during 1967. The whole batch when transferred to the WYPTE had their original numbers pre-fixed by the figure 4. Here KVH 473E is caught wearing the simplified livery on the route 323 at the top of Alandale Road, Bradley.*
Robert Berry Collection

Yet the-powers-that-be quickly over-turned this concession to local tradition and imposed on all constituent fleets the green version of Leeds. Also lost were the individual fleet-names with all constituent fleets later sharing a uniform West Yorkshire Passenger Transport Executive (PTE) corporate name and livery.

With the coming of this new age of reasonably efficient (but impersonal) PTEs, all was not lost. Although Huddersfield Corporation Passenger Transport Department, ceased to exist after operation on 31st March 1974, it did not vanish overnight. Even after 91-years 2-months and 20-days of municipal pride, one could still see a few buses standing proud and defiant in their Huddersfield livery.

Although Huddersfield Corporation Transport Department did not see its centenary of municipal bus operation, Metro Bus celebrated the occasion as a public relations exercise in 1983. They did this by re-painting two of their 1980-1 Roe-bodied Leyland Atlanteans. Of these 6299 (PUA 299W) was painted into the Huddersfield JOC livery with the proclamation '100 Years of Public Transport' below the upper-deck windows, whilst 6300 (PUA 300W) was painted in the old tramway livery of maroon and ivory.

In conclusion we must mention the two large garages owned by the Corporation, and from where the buses were operated. The first of these was at Great Northern Street, which also had an entry onto Leeds Road This was the original Huddersfield Tramways Depot as lettering in the stone portico above the building proudly proclaimed. Directly adjacent to the town's Monday Market and alongside the Fitzwilliam Street with its steam-operated gasworks railway, this was always a Mecca for young boys interested in transport.

The other, newer depot was alongside the River Colne at Longroyd Bridge, and had originally been designed for the new trolley buses. The fleets were largely segregated between the two depots prior to 1969, with the Corporation vehicles being at Longroyd Bridge and the JOC buses at Great Northern Street, which was sadly demolished a few short years ago.

Below: *Among the single deck buses in the JOC fleet were a pair of Leyland Leopard L1 models which had been delivered during 1961. These Roe-bodied saloons were given the fleet numbers 21-2 (SCX 21-2), and were intended for the more rural routes. Both vehicles survived in stock down to the end of the undertaking and therefore passed to the West Yorkshire PTE. During the period of trying to achieve a certain form of standardisation among the constituent members of the WYPTE, this pair (along with various other Leylands) were later transferred to the Halifax area. Upon withdrawal from fare stage service, SCX 22 found itself in a further livery variation, when it was transferred to the Driver Training fleet. Here former 22, now T6, is seen in the locality of the Halifax bus station.*
Robert Berry Collection

BADDELEY BROTHERS (OLYMPIA MOTOR SERVICES, GREEN & WHITE)

Hiram Baddeley of Emley, was reputedly the first man in that area to run a motorcar when he was supplied with one by the owners of the mines he was the manager for. This was to enable him to fulfil his duties more efficiently. Sadly he was killed when involved in a mining accident in 1908 near Skelmenthorpe, leaving a widow (Florence) and four children. The family first moved to Moldgreen then later to a house on Somerset Road, Almondbury. The sons, Jesse and Leonard Baddeley were respectively just 19 and 17 years old when, towards the end of 1918, they took over the operation of a relative's garage. This was the Olympia Motor Works, at Fieldhouse, just off Leeds Road, where they started with a locally-built Karrier lorry. One of their earliest jobs was hauling bricks for the Leeds Fireclay Company, who had a works near to the garage. Early in 1919 a friend, Ai Earnshaw, who also ran a haulage company in Huddersfield suggested to Jesse that he might like to buy a charabanc body to put on the lorry, as there was a growing need for motorbus trips now that the war had ended.

Top Left: *One of two ex-Wallace Arnold, AEC Reliance 2MU3RA models with early versions of Plaxton Panorama bodywork were taken into the Baddeley Brothers fleet during 1969, and mainly used on workmans' services.*
Robert Berry Collection

Bottom Left: *The rear view of 102, (9303 NW) shows the "Prince of Wales' feathers that had become part of the insignia as far back as 1935. This AEC Reliance 2MU3RA model was one of a pair that were new to Wallace Arnold of Leeds in 1959.* Robert Berry Collection

Top Right: *Baddeley Brothers 100, was a 1962 Bedford SB5 with Plaxton bodywork. Seen here standing alongside a Bedford VAL in Holmfirth. Purchased second-hand in 1969, GCU 574 was one of the vehicles in the fleet at the time of the West Yorks PTE take over in March 1976*
Robert Berry Collection

By the summer of 1919, Jesse and Leonard were doing a roaring trade with their tours, but as this was seasonal work, Baddeley's began to look to new areas of business and by 1920 they were running a timetabled bus service between Huddersfield and Brighouse. During 1921 the brothers had also concluded a deal with Holmfirth Urban District Council to operate a service linking the tram terminus at Honley with Holmbridge

In March 1924, Baddeley's were granted a bus stand in the town's High Street, and they gained another tram extension service from the terminus at Lockwood through to Meltham in October 1921. This was again thanks to Ai Earnshaw, who had persuaded the Meltham Urban District Council to licence a motor bus service to compete with the newly merged L&YR/LNWR railway, who had announced an increase of prices to take effect from 1st January 1922. Prior to the coming of the railway, a relative of the Earnshaw's had operated the horse-bus service to Huddersfield.

Although Meltham UDC welcomed the bus service, Huddersfield Corporation made it clear that Baddeley's would just have a stewardship for the route as far as the Borough boundary at Netherton Bar. They also added that when they decided to run buses on that route, they would expect Baddeley to withdraw. When the Corporation started running to Meltham in 1924, the two operators had a seemingly peaceful co-existence, yet in March 1925 the battle between the Corporation and Baddeley began again, especially when the Corporation put extra buses on the Meltham route.

Increased pressure from the Corporation bus services and competition from other independent companies brought about severe financial difficulties for Baddeley Brothers. Jesse and Leonard's sister, Miss Florence Adella Baddeley proved her acumen as a teacher of mathematics by taking charge of the company books. It is said that she overcame the stubbornness of her brothers, and with a family friend who was a solicitor, negotiated a deal in July 1925 to sell Olympia Motor Services and its routes to the Corporation.

This was not to be the end of Baddeley Brothers though as after the sale of the company Leonard turned his sights on the small market town of Holmfirth. From there, with his brother, mother, and sister as co-directors, Leonard started trading under the new company name of Green & White; this fleet-name adored the flanks of the company vehicles for the next ten years. In 1926 licenses were obtained for new routes from Holmfirth to Penistone and Dunford Bridge, other routes were later established, and by the early 1930s Baddeley Brothers were also running over a dozen excursion destinations too.

With the appointment of Guy Levison as manager in 1935 the coaching side of the business was quickly expanded.

An almost-new coach was purchased' this being a 1934 Albion Valiant (BV 3505), with a luxury 32-seat body. This was to be known as a 'Land Cruiser' and it was with this coach that the company adopted the Prince of Wales plumes as a trade mark. However the service buses were painted, as the fleet name suggests, in a green and white livery. Meanwhile to emphasise the growing commitment to the luxury tours business, a new livery was adopted for the front line touring coaches. This used black for the roof area, with the lower bodywork in an ivory and green streamlined colour scheme.

Further expansion took place in July 1936 with the purchase of Beaumont Brothers coach business at Meltham. This was the year that Ai Earnshaw died and his family sold their stables to Beaumonts to build a motor dealers garage on Huddersfield Road. To finance the purchase, Beamonts offered their bus operation to Baddeleys. Only one of their two vehicles was involved in the sale, but further excursion licenses were included, and these were added to the ones already granted by the Traffic Commissioners. Coaching expansion continued to develop throughout the late-1930s, but as elsewhere in the country this recreational activity was brought to a complete halt during the war, whilst normal stage services were also consequently reduced with the workmen's journeys taking priority. Three Bedford OWB models were purchased during the war years to help maintain these essential workers services.

Although wartime restrictions had been eased somewhat during the latter part of 1945, it was not until 1946 that the firm reached something like its pre-war normality. The fleet which stood at 23 buses and coaches, still consisted mainly of the pre-war models, yet with these time-served vehicles the majority of the pre-war tours were re-established, and the excursion program (which had its restrictions lifted for Easter 1946) was rapidly fully booked.

During this time the fleet still retained the green and white livery for the service buses, but the excursion coaches were now in a dual green and white colour scheme. During 1947, Leonard Baddeley became seriously ill, and as his brother Jesse had died early in November 1931 at the age of 32, management of the firm became a problem. As Florence had not married, Leonard began looking around for a man to take charge of the business. He eventually appointed John Thomas Steel, a qualified engineer with considerable experience in the coaching industry. When Leonard died on 10th October 1947, Mr. Steel took up his new position with the company the following day, while Miss Baddeley became the chairman of the company.

Baddeley Brothers' operations were extremely varied with fare stage routes, several workmen services, contracts for school services in Holmfirth, Meltham and Penistone, as well as excursions and private-hire work. The appointment of Mr. Steel as manager proved to be extremely justified, for here was a man who was to prove to be completely committed to the company. It is a reflection on him and the staff that the company is still locally held in high esteem for the caring and reliable service that they provided.

While at the Earls Court Commercial Motor Show in 1950, Mr. Steel was extremely impressed by the revolutionary new Leyland under-floor engine chassis, and he arranged the purchase of one with the impressive new Burlingham Seagull style of bodywork by Burlingham, This vehicle, which was delivered in 1951 and given fleet number 50 (KWU 844), was the *crème de la crème* in luxury coach standards at that time.

Above: *Baddeley No. 118 (MUG 522L), was a 1973 Leyland Leopard PSU3B/4R with Plaxton Panorama Elite body. This is one of the vehicles bought by West Yorkshire PTE to replenish the fleet's time-served vehicles.* H. John Black.

Another example was delivered in 1953 but this later coach, 52 (LWY 653), had the MkII Seagull style, employing in its design what was to be known as the 'double tank flash'. It is believed that No.50 was the first vehicle to be painted in the company's simplified livery of two shades of green without any white relief. Among the other buses and coaches to enter the fleet in the 1950s, was number 55. This was unusual, as it was a double-deck bus, DTD 169 (No.55), which was a 1938 Leyland Titan TD5, with low-bridge bodywork by Massey that had been new to Leigh Corporation.

For many years Baddeleys had operated taxis and a well-respected funeral service alongside their bus and coach business. On parallel operating lines, was the sometimes-difficult relationship with a rival company, G.W. Castle, also based in Holmfirth. When it was learnt that this company was to close down their coaching side of the business in 1966 in favour of expanding their funeral, taxi and car dealership enterprises, John Steel arranged a meeting with its directors . The outcome of this was to prove beneficial for both concerns, for when Castle's surrendered their excursion licenses, similar ones were

successfully obtained by Baddeleys along with one of Castle's five coaches (HCX 491). In return the taxi and funeral side of Baddeley's business passed into the hands of the Castle Brothers.

The formation of the West Yorkshire PTE had a devastating effect on smaller operators who could not hope to compete with the financial backing of such enterprises. When (in May 1974) Hanson's coaches were acquired, the PTE announced that the fleet was to be modernised with a large number of new Volvo coaches, the writing was on the wall for Baddeleys. It therefore came as no great surprise when, on 24th March 1976, Baddeleys lost their independence and suffered the indifference of a ruling body in distant Leeds. However, a condition of the sale saw the Baddeley livery being retained for a while, and as a result the PTE introduced new vehicles in this colour scheme.

HANSON OF HUDDERSFIELD

Among the many pioneering businesses in Huddersfield, was the company of Joseph Hanson & Son. This enterprise took over an old established horse-drawn haulage business and was registered as a limited company on 25th September 1920. It was in due course, to become one of the country's largest long-distance haulage contractors. I have a close affinity with

Hansons, as my father was a body-builder for them at the Leeds Road site in the 1960s, whilst my editor's grandfather (Ai Earnshaw) sold his haulage business to the family in the 1930s, despite the fact his business had once employed twice as many horses and wagons than were found in the Hanson operation. Others will recognise the Hanson name from the smart, modern fleet of road vehicles connected with the brick-making, cement and aggregate industries.

Left: *Hanson buses and their sombre deep red livery, were world famous (to school-boys in Huddersfield anyway). This enterprising company had an enviable reputation for re-building time-served vehicles and then having new bodywork fitted at the Roe factory at Crossgates near Leeds. This AEC Regent NVH 399 (350) was just one example.* H. John Black

Top Right *Here SCX 543, stands in the old bus station on a special service. Very subtle differences could be found in the eight Regal re-builds with their full-front saloon bodywork. Compare 360 with 377 below.* H. John Black

Bottom Right: *Hanson's 377 was the last of eight similar Roe-bodied buses that had been re-built from time served AEC Regal chassis and components. Here XVH 135 basks in the sun on a warm day at Lindley before embarking on its journey to Milnsbridge* H. John Black

The company diversified into bus and coach services, using vehicles painted in a livery of ivory and dark red during the late-1920s. This then became a separate operational business and Hanson's Buses became a registered limited company on 15th April 1935, although they were still based at the company's road haulage premises in Milnsbridge at this time.

Hanson's Haulage was one of the first to be voluntarily sold to the British Transport Commission in 1948 with the setting up of a national transport industry. However, the part of their fleet contracted to the Imperial Chemical Industries, both at their Manchester base and their Woodlands Road garage just off Leeds Road in Huddersfield, was retained. The livery for this contract fleet was painted in a petrol blue colour and lettered ICI (Dyestuff Division).

The parent haulage fleet used a medium red livery with the Hanson name in large gold letters on the sides. Following the de-nationalisation of road haulage in 1952, the fleet was re-established in 1955 and considerably expanded, using a base at a different site on Leeds Road.

A large garage (with excellent maintenance workshops on St. John's Road), later became the depot for the (by then) dark red-painted bus and coach fleet. From here services were operated all over the Huddersfield area, some of which were jointly run with the JOC. Hansons also operated an independent 'Trans-Pennine' service, through the Colne Valley to Oldham.

Several local coach companies were acquired over the years by Hanson, including Bottomley Motors in 1951. Chapman's, Ivy Coaches were acquired in 1953, and then in 1962, the Marsden-based company of W H & F Schofield. The firm of Bottomley Motors was retained as a separate coaching subsidiary until 1962, with coaches still using Bottomley's two-tone blue livery. Even in later years, isolated new coaches for the Hanson fleet were delivered in an overall dark blue livery, featuring the Bottomley name in gold script on the sides.

For both coaches and service buses, Hansons had long favoured the AEC chassis, although Bedford, Maudsley and other chassis had also been purchased. Bodywork was of a largely conservative nature, with the products of Charles Roe chosen for the service buses. Meanwhile coach bodies came from Plaxton of Scarborough, but other examples of bodybuilders had been used from time to time. For instance, various Duple designs had been bought, among them XVH 136-9 and BCX 488-91B, which were 1963 and 1964 examples of the 37-seat Firefly model; these coaches were all on Ford chassis.

For several years, an interesting aspect of this company, was the re-building of some of their older AEC Regent and Regal chassis to eight-foot width in their own workshops! These were then fitted with new bodies by Charles Roe, either half-cab double-deck or as full-front 39-seat, front-entrance single-deckers with AEC Regent V type radiator grills. Included in these rebuilds were Regal IIIs, NCX 367/481, SCX 543, TVH 498-9, VVH 349 and XVH 134-5.

Top Right: *The local coaching concern of Bottomley Motors was acquired by Hanson in 1951. This was run as a subsidiary until 1962 with several coaches painted in Bottomley's blue livery. Yet even when this side of the business was fully absorbed, Hanson continued to paint isolated coaches in a uniform dark blue colour scheme with the Bottomley name in gold script adorning the sides. Ford Thames coach 392 (ECX 110C), was one of four identical Plaxton-bodied coaches delivered in 1965. Sister vehicles 393-5 wore the red livery of Hanson coaches. H. John Black.*

Bottom Right: *Parked across the road from the Hanson garage and workshops in St. Johns Road, this coach (KVH 295E) appears to be in need of a little first aid. Coach 404, a Duple-bodied Ford R192, along with sister vehicle to the Hanson fleet, 403, (KVH 296E), were new in 1967. H. John Black.*

Top Left: *This Ford chassis was bodied by Plaxton in 1962, and as VVH 189 it became fleet number 371. It still retains the white side flash that was carried on the earlier Hanson livery, but as coachbodies started to appear with extra chrome trim, it was decided to drop this flash in the early-1960s.* H. John Black.

Bottom Left: *Another Ford chassis is this Thames Trader with 1965 Plaxton Panorama bodywork. Identical to 392 seen in the Bottomley livery on page 35, this became 394.* H. John Black.

The picture of the Bottomley Ford Duple on the previous page, and the similar Viceroy body on the AEC opposite remind me of a curious story, as I am currently restoring a Ford Duple Viceroy JEK 31H. For this vehicle was for a short time in the Hanson fleet, as Colin Carlyle recalls.

"In 1972 I brought the Bottomley-liveried Ford R226/Viceroy back from Blackpool Illuminations, and as we came down Outlands towards Huddersfield it ground to a halt. The prop-shaft had broke. Fortunately the floor wasn't penetrated. However this was a Friday night trip, but it was Honley Feast, a local holiday, so all bus drivers were being used. The passengers were transferred to another Hanson bus and taken home. The next morning I went to the dealers Hughes of Cleckheaton to pick up a replacement, and we chose another R226 with a MkII Viceroy body – none other than JEK 31H. We had that bus for several months, and I recall doing a trip to Newton Aycliffe with a local school football team who were playing in a youth cup match.

A few weeks later the coach went back to Hughes, but I came across it in the spring of 1973 when it was working, on loan, with Lyle's of Batley, then I parked up against it in Scarborough at Whitsuntide when it was on loan to Anderton's of Bingley. We had it back at Hanson for about six weeks in the summer of 1973, and used it quite a lot of the time.

Nobody wanted Viceroys then as the new Dominants were coming out, and the Viceroy was dated and also very stuffy due to all that glass. There was talk that it could be bought very reasonably, and I was asked to take our chief engineer for a spin up the M62 to Windy Hill. I was to drive out while he watched how it performed, and then he would drive it back.

Those Fords were slow beggars at climbing the hills, but when we were on the climb past Scammonden Dam, I knew something was wrong, because the vehicle kept pulling to the kerb, and I fought with it all the way. Then the front wheels locked up and she slewed across the road and wiped out an emergency telephone. The side panels were ripped off amidships, and the engineer had seen enough. Back it went to Hughes, with some choice words."

As the Hanson empire began to expand, the bus fleet became a smaller part of the overall operation, and with the service buses ageing, a decision was taken to move out of this area and concentrate on the coaching side of the business.

Accordingly, Huddersfield Corporation acquired the operational routes and the 23-strong fleet of service buses on 1st October 1969. The newest of these were three AEC Reliance buses with dual-purpose Willowbrook bodies, which were bought new in 1967/8. After this Hanson continued to operate as a coaching business until this side of the business was taken over by the West Yorkshire PTE. as mentioned in the chapter on Baddeley Brothers.

Top Right: *Ford Transits first made their debut in 1965, and proved so popular as commercials and PSVs that within a short time they were the market leader in their class. Parked in the vicinity of the new Huddersfield bus station is Hanson's GVH 287L. H. John Black.*

Bottom Right: *Sister vehicle to 404 the Bottomley coach on page 35, displays the more artistic and true front end of these Duple coaches. KVH 296E, is at the same location. H. John Black.*

OTHER STAGE CARRIAGE OPERATORS

As mentioned in our introduction, Huddersfield like a cut (but un-polished diamond) was a town of many facets, including some superb architecture. But in addition to the diversity of its buildings, it may surprise some readers to note the dirvesity of the bus fleets that once served the district, as this is such a contrast to the present day.

We have discussed the two main independents and the twin fleets of Huddersfield Corporation and the JOC, but thus far have not mentioned the bus stations or stands within the town. Up to the building of a new overall bus station at Macaullay Street in the early 1970s (into which the majority of services were diverted), bus routes started and terminated either at Upperhead Row or at stands on the town's streets.

Above: *Although the Upperhead Row bus stations were to the west of the town, and the railway station to the east, bus stands were found all along the connecting streets. Laid out in a 'square grid' pattern, the street plan gave thoroughfares at right-angles to one another. The area in front of the railway station, St.George's Square, was left 'open' with grand buildings surrounding it. One of these buildings was the Lion Arcade on John William Street, which is seen with its stone lion above the buses furthest from the camera. Beyond this the soot-stained building at the corner of Northumberland Street housed the Corporation's Passenger Transport Department office. The front bus is a Halifax Leyland of 1965 vintage waiting to depart on Route 42, but it looks considerably more antiquated than the 1966 Huddersfield Daimler behind it on Route 14 to Holmfirth via Oldfield.* Strathwood Library

Top Right: *During 1965, ten of these Leyland Titan PD2/37 models (fitted with front-entrance 64-seat bodies by Weymann), entered the Halifax JOC fleet.* H. John Black

Bottom Right: *Whilst this is not a high quality picture, it serves to illustrate how the Halifax livery appeared after a number of years service. Not only has the picture slightly faded, but so too has the paintwork on this 1951 AEC Regent III 9613E model. The Park Royal bodywork has a slight resemblance to the bodies fitted to London Transport RT models produced by this same manufacturer.* Robert Berry Collection

Upperhead Row bus station was divided into two halves, and was mainly used by the JOC, Hansons and Baddeleys, whilst the Corporation trolley buses (which operated cross-town services), would stop at stands on the main thoroughfares or outside the railway station in St. George's Square. Byram Street, New Street, John William Street, High Street, Kirkgate, Westgate, Market Street and Northumberland Street were the other main locations for stands.

Buses from the fleet of the Sheffield JOC visited Huddersfield too, and these would stand on Lord Street (near the junction with Kirkgate), whilst working the limited stop X68 service. This long run between Sheffield and Halifax was jointly operated with Yorkshire Traction.

Near neighbour, Halifax Corporation had (since 12th October 1925) been undertaking joint workings on the routes to Huddersfield. These routes ran via the smaller towns of Elland or West Vale, and were numbered 42 and 43. They shared a lot of common ground when they left Huddersfield, passing through the suburbs of Edgerton and Birchencliffe. They then gently climbed to Ainley Top before plunging down the winding valley to Elland, where they would separate. One climbed up Victoria Road, then followed the valley side down to West Vale, while the other wandered through the centre of Elland to Elland Bridge, with both joining again for the common route up Salterhebble Hill.

Top Left: *Waiting outside the Halifax Building Society offices in Halifax, we see the first of the nine Leyland Royal Tiger Worldmaster buses that were delivered to Halifax Corporation in 1958. This batch of Weymann-bodied saloons were registered KCP 1-9, and numbered accordingly.* Robert Berry Collection

Bottom Left: *Here number 51 (TCP 51), a 1963 Leyland Titan, stands in Huddersfield while working on Route 43. Joint working on these routes had started on 12th October 1925, but Halifax also had joint arrangements with other neighbouring municipalities, including a moorland route across to Rochdale that had started in 1926.* H. John Black

Halifax, in very many ways, was similar to Huddersfield, as it nestled in a deep valley, so all the roads go up- or down-hill and even the bus station was on a tilt. Like, Leeds, Bradford, and Huddersfield, Halifax considered the operation of trolleybuses as a replacement for its tramway system and for a short time in the 1920s actually operated a small, very small network.

However, this did not prove very satisfactory and thereafter motorbuses were used. Reputedly a Leyland Titan TD1, was demonstrated in Halifax, before it was delivered to the City of Glasgow, (other sources claim that it was an early Regent), and this influenced a distinctive new livery for the fleet. Impressed with Glasgow's livery, the Transport Department decided to adopt a similar colour, but used a deeper shade of orange to highlight the green and cream and employed a slightly different method of application. After this they consigned their previous Indian Red and white livery to the history books.

Halifax was another municipal bus operator who entered into agreement with the LMS railway to set-up a joint omnibus committee, which came into being on 1st April 1929. One of the first signs of this new agreement was to assign the joint route from Halifax to Rochdale to the new JOC committee.

While Halifax was a very industrial town, the surrounding area was very rural. The early years of my life were spent in the very rural hamlet of Blackley, high on the watershed above Elland. In the absence of a family car, the single-deck buses of Halifax were our only form of transport at the time.

Halifax was to become one of the constituent parts of the West Yorkshire PTE. and to facilitate this it merged with the municipal fleet of Todmorden to form Calderdale. Around this time a certain form of vehicle rationalisation was also seen to take place. With the transfer of vehicles, each district was more able to standardise on certain chassis. For instance Huddersfield's AECs were noted to be serving at Bradford, whilst some of their Leylands went to Halifax.

The formation of the PTE also affected route operation and my editor was a member (and later became Vice-Chair) of the West Yorkshire Passenger User's Consultative Committee. During his tenure he had lengthy battles to protect many passenger services in the area following bus de-regulation.

Although the Halifax livery was phased out by the mid-1970s, several preserved buses kept it alive. A number of these were later operated on 'Heritage Services' by Tony Blackman, on several routes in or around Calderdale. This operation eventually grew in to a stage-carriage business, for which Tony and his family 'naturally' kept the old Halifax colour scheme.

Top Right: *Halifax Corporation was very traditional and kept purchasing exposed-radiator models until the mid-1960s, such as this Leyland Titan PD2/37, with Weymann bodywork. Robert Berry Collection*

Bottom Right: *During the 1920s Halifax had tended to choose Daimler, Dennis and Karrier chassis for its bus fleet. With the end of production of front-engined models in the mid-1960s, it decided to revert to Daimler once again, choosing their rear-engined Fleetline model. Robert Berry Collection*

Various works buses and coaches were also to be found in the centre of Huddersfield too, for many of the large companies found it practical to collect and return their workforce, using contract services supplied by one of the established operators; examples of such operations included Mackintosh's Toffee from Halifax and Fox's Biscuits from Batley, who both used private hire operators. Some firms purchased their own vehicle(s) and used a member of staff as driver. Among the companies to do this were Brook Electric Motors, T.W. Broadbent and the BBC who used two small coaches in their corporate livery for the transport of their staff to the rather isolated transmitter stations at Holme Moss and Pole Moor.

One works bus that I recall seeing in Huddersfield was a 1960 Leyland Leopard with the very attractive Harrington Cavalier coachwork. This vehicle (6692 KH) was often to be found in St. George's square, and although I did not discover the owner of this coach, which was painted lemon and red; it had been new to East Yorkshire Motor Services

Summer season was an absolute hive of activity, as a flotilla of coaches constantly departed from Upperhead Row taking the masses to established holiday haunts, or ferried them back and forth on day excursions. At this time the local coach companies were jostling for road space with Abbeyways and Ivesways (both of Halifax), Wallace Arnold of Leeds, and various interlopers from Lancashire. One of the most commonly seen operators from over the Pennines was Yelloways of Rochdale. This firm often hired vehicles to both Baddeleys and Hansons, but they also had a pick-up point in Huddersfield for some of their own long-distance services.

Below: *It is still possible to view Huddersfield railway station from this vantage point, but the scene has been considerably improved by the demolition of the bus shelters and the cleaning of the station buildings. The unusual occupant of the bus stand is SGD 669, a Leyland Atlantean demonstrator with 78-seat bodywork by Alexander.* Strathwood Library

Running parallel to, but below John William Street, seen in so many of the pictures thus far, were two other streets on which a large number of bus stands were located. These were Byram Street and Lord Street. Operators from 'outside the area' were concentrated on these streets, but they also housed services operated by Corporation and JOC vehicles. For instance Byram Street hosted the stands for the Yorkshire Woollen District route to Leeds via. Heckmondwyke or Dewsbury, and the Corporation's Almondbury route the Hanson stand for Weatherhill.

Lord Street, was the Huddersfield terminal for a number of operators, including County Motors, Hebble (later West Yorkshire), Sheffield JOC, West Riding, Yorkshire Traction, and Huddersfield.

Above: *As we will discuss later, Route 64 between Bradford and Huddersfield was actually a joint operation on which the West Yorkshire Road Car Company took over from Hebble following restructuring of the National Bus Company routes in 1970. Here a Bristol Lodekka with Eastern Counties bodywork, DYG 222B (DX 182), is found in its original livery whilst standing in Lord Street.* H. John Black

Meanwhile nearby Venn Street was the location for most of the long-distance services, and was the place where you could see (at various times), vehicles from Lancashire United, Northern General, North Western Road Car and United Automobiles to name but a few.

The enormous West Yorkshire Road Car operation, which dates from 1st January 1928, was formed when the Harrogate & District Road Car Company changed its title. It became the West Yorkshire Road Car after the acquisition of Blythe & Berwick of Bradford. Harrogate & District had commenced operations in December 1906, with services in Harrogate and Knaresborough, using a small fleet of single-deck Clarkson steam buses. Very little expansion took place until a controlling interest in the company was taken by Thomas Tilling and BAT in 1924. Premier Transport of Keighley was acquired in 1926. Then in 1932 and 1934, the municipal fleets of Keighley and York were taken over to respectively form Keighley-West Yorkshire and York-West Yorkshire.

Above: *Here we see XWW 472G, one of the first series of the well respected and now sadly missed Bristol VR models. In its pre-NCB livery, we find it at rest outside the YMCA premises on Lord Street, Huddersfield.* H. John Black

West Yorkshire did not find its way to Huddersfield by a stage-carriage route until after the formation of NCB after the 1968 Transport Act. As a result of a rationalisation of services it acquired a share in the Route 64 service from Bradford to Huddersfield from Hebble, as we will discuss. The arrival of West Yorkshire vehicles introduced to Huddersfield the combination of Bristol chassis and ECW bodies, which were not widely seen on stage carriage services in the town prior to that.

This route which passed through Brighouse, Bailiff Bridge and Wyke, was still numbered 12 in the early 1950s and at one time operated on a 15-minute frequency. I fondly recall the ECW bodied Bristol Lodekka FS models, bowling along Bradford Road 20-years later.

However, coaches from this fleet had been seen on long-distance services calling at Venn Street for a number of years, including Bristol MW models with ECW coachwork. On occasions I have even seen FWW 596, the firm's solitary Bedford OB. This Duple-bodied coach was rather unusual, for it was built in 1947 with cant-rail lights, (curved windows in the roof) and was intended for York City sight-seeing tours. What made it unusual was the fact that at the time of its acquisition, it was the only none-Bristol chassis in the whole fleet of some 500 + buses and coaches.

Top Right: *Before the building of the new Huddersfield bus station, the majority of fare stage services terminated at stands in the various thoroughfares of the town. Waiting to return to Bradford on Route 64 via Brighouse, Bailiff Bridge and Wyke, we see West Yorkshire's DX 153 (277 BWU). This is another one of the classic Bristol FS6B models with ECW H33/27RD bodywork. As it waits in Lord Street, the photographer has captured the rather cumbersome-looking intakes of the Cave-Brown-Cave, heating and ventilation system on the front panel above the driver. This is the only distraction from the harmonious lines of these attractive buses. H. John Black*

Bottom Right: *Customers who adhered faithfully to Bristol chassis, chose the VR model in the era of high capacity, O-M-O operation. But, as with all new things, when introduced it met with a slight reservation from operators of traditional buses. Yet in its later Series II and III forms, it became one of the most highly regarded chassis, and nationally popular with both bus operators and the travelling public alike. H. John Black*

The baby blue and milky cream double-deck buses of Bradford Corporation were also participants on the Huddersfield-Bradford service, running via Brighouse. In earlier days, Brighouse had been the change-over point between the two undertakings, but the tram journey by this route was far quicker than the railway route via Mirfield and the Spen Valley. It was the last route on which Huddersfield trams had run, but these came to an end in the dark days of 1940. Bradford started to abandon its trams as early as November 1928, when the city purchased its first double-deck motor buses, however it was not until 6th May 1950 that the last tram ran. Bradford was also noted for its extensive trolley bus system, with the inaugural opening ceremony taking place on 20th June 1911. This was also the last operational trolleybus system in Britain, but that is beyond the scope of this book.

Bradford City transport favoured Leyland and AEC chassis for their bus fleet during the 1960s, although Daimler also found favour from time to time. Bradford's fleet by the way consisted almost entirely of double-deck buses, with just two AEC Reliance saloons breaking the monopoly.

Top Left: *Bradford purchased several batches of the AEC Regent V model, some of which were quite large. One example was 167 (2167 KW) as this was one of a batch of 60 ordered in 1963. They were fitted with 70-seat bodies by Metro-Cammell, a further 30 similar models arrived the following year. H. John Black*

Bottom Left: *When Bradford embarked on fleet renewal in the late-1960s, they started buying rear-engined buses. Modern buses like this Daimler Fleetline (PKW 426J) were thus taken into stock. This example is bodied by Alexander as can be seen from alternative styling treatment of roof, window design and sculptured lower front panels; making them a refreshing change from the rather bland offerings of other bodybuilders. H. John Black*

As mentioned earlier, the Bradford services were partially operated by the Hebble company, who had garages in both Halifax and Bradford. This company had been started by two brothers (Oliver and Charles Holdsworth), who were well known hauliers in Halifax. Joined by their nephew, Norman Dean, they began the Hebble Bus Company on 1st December 1924. Early services were operated to Brighouse via Southowram and also to Bingley via Denholme.

Services started running from Commercial Street, Halifax, but it was not until 1927 that a garage was finally acquired; this was situated in Walnut Street. Prior to this accommodation and maintenance for the fleet of buses was carried out in the depot of Holdsworth Haulage in Halifax. Expansion began in 1925 with services to Greetland (and later to Elland), but this route was soon extended to Huddersfield. Further expansion took place in 1928 with the purchase of the services and vehicles of Hugh Brigg of Wilsden.

Although Hebble continued to rise in status, their days as an independant operator came to an end in April 1929 when the Holdsworth Brothers sold the business to the LMS Railway, although Norman Dean still remained with the company as General Manager. Expansion continued throughout the pre-war years with a great increase in contract and excursion work.

Top Right: *Although Valiant chassis had been used by Hebble in the early years, Leyland and AEC chassis were favoured later. Here we see NCP 475, one of a pair of Metro-Cammell-bodied AEC Regent Vs that were new in 1960.* H. John Black

Bottom Right: *After the 1968 Transport Act, when Hebble passed to the NBC, all of their stage-carriage services were given to other operators; the majority going to Halifax JOC. In the new National Travel coach livery, this 1966 AEC Reliance with a Duple body passes through Huddersfield on the way to Blackpool.* H. John Black

Further excursion expansion came during the 1950s with the take over of three coach operators, including Ripponden & District in 1957, which brought a further 11 coaches into the fleet. The following year the business of Walton & Helliwell was acquired. This was partly owned by the original founders of Hebble, the Holdsworth Brothers, who had re-entered the coaching business after the sale of Hebble to the LMS, who (in turn) had sold a 50% share to British Electric Traction.

When the National Bus Company was formed, it took over the BET bus interests and decided to rationalise the structure of the various bus companies in West Yorkshire. It actually created three groups, which were all controlled from a main office in Wakefield these were West Riding, Yorkshire Woollen District and Hebble.

From this reconstruction, Hebble became the principle coaching operator having the bulk of the stage services transferred to Halifax JOC, but its third share in Route 64 between Huddersfield and Bradford passed to West Yorkshire. From 1971 Hebble was only a partner in the newly formed Yorkshire Woollen District/Hebble coach services, which were based at Frost Hill in Liversedge. This later became National Travel (North-East), after which the Hebble name was only to be seen on preserved buses.

Below: *Hebble 277 (PCP 403), was one of four AEC Regent V buses delivered in 1962. It displays the handsome lines of its Northern Counties' bodywork as it waits in Lord Street.* John Black

Another long-established fleet that terminated on Lord Street, was West Riding Automobile Company who had commenced operations as the Wakefield & District Light Railway Company in 1905. The newer title had been adopted for a subsidiary during 1922 to operate motor buses, but this was wound up in 1935 and the parent company then adopted the title. During the late-1950s, this was still an independent company. Although Guy chassis had been the choice for double-deck buses since 1955, Leyland had been the preferred choice in the pre-war years. They operated Guy Arab, Leyland Titan PD2, or Guy Wulfrunian double-deckers in the 1960s.

Above: *West-Riding operated from four depots; Wakefield ,Featherstone , Castleford and Selby. However, as the name suggests the 400 + strong fleet operated all over the West Riding. Guy Motors developed their Wolfrunian model in conjunction with the West Riding Automobile Company, and with this company nearly every single example of this type eventually operated. New in 1966, EHL 694D, was one of 25 Leyland Atlantean PDR1/2 models; these were built with Roe bodies. Behind bus 107, stands one of the 1955/6 Guy Arab Mk.IV models. these were also fitted with Roe bodies, but to a low-bridge design.*

When we come to the services operated to the south and south west of Huddersfield, we have a minor dilemma, as we are saving a number of Yorkshire Traction and County Motors pictures for a future book. Yet, it is obvious that we must include them in this narrative, as they were a regular sight in the town. Yorkshire Traction was formed in 1902 as the Barnsley & District Electric Traction Company to operate tramcars, but changed their name in 1928. For many years, most of this 350+ strong fleet was of Leyland manufacture, scattered among its six garages. One of these was a small depot in Lincoln Street, just off St. Andrews Road near Holsett Engineering in Huddersfield.

The largest municipal fleet in the West Riding of Yorkshire was Leeds City, but Leeds and Huddersfield had no joint service agreement. Accordingly Yorkshire Woollen District provided the services between Leeds and Huddersfield operating through Dewsbury or via the Spen Valley towns. There were many other fascinating bus and coach fleets also serving West Yorkshire at this time some of whom may have had coaches pass through or near Huddersfield on private hire, such as Joseph Woods of Mirfield, or J. J. Longstaff, both of whom also operated a fare stage between the towns of Mirfield and Dewsbury.

Top Left: *Yorkshire Traction was for decades a staunch Leyland customer, operating examples of just about every model of single deck and double deck-models produced. After sampling early Atlantean models in 1959, further examples of this chassis followed as this 1966 model shows.* Strathwood Library

Bottom Left: *The Yorkshire Woollen District Transport Company based at Saville Town, Dewsbury had much more variety in its fleet. This company who operated stage services linking Leeds and Huddersfield, chose both Daimler Fleetline and Leyland Atlantean chassis, often bodied by Alexander.* Strathwood Library

The third principle operator to use Lord Street as a terminus was another Huddersfield company, who were based just off Wakefield Road at Waterloo. This was County Motors, which had been started by a consortium of local businessmen in the early 1920s, but was now partially owned by West Riding and operated routes to Grange Moor, Dewsbury, Wakefield and Barnsley. The fleet livery had at one time been deep blue and cream, but this was later changed to ivory and two shades of blue; it was later simplified again to just ivory and the paler shade of blue.

In the early post-war years, Guy Arab double-deck buses were favoured, with Leyland chassis the long standing choice for saloons. An interesting pair of 1949 Leyland Tiger PS2s were EVH 213-4, which had Windover full-front coach bodies fitted in 1954. One of these was later sold for use as a staff bus by the local engineering firm of T.W. Broadbent. Serving alongside the double-deck Guys, were a couple of 1952 Leyland Titan PD2/12s.

Like their parent company, West Riding, Guy Wulfrunians were later bought and registered as UCX 275-6 and bodied by Roe. Although these were bought in 1961, they did not prove very successful and were sold to West Riding in 1963. They were replaced by a handsome pair of Leyland Titan PD3As, (AVH 635-6B) in 1964, while the single-deck fleet was regularly updated by successive Leyland models.

Top Right: *A scene inside the garage at Waterloo, Huddersfield, Fleet number 389 has a 1962 Willowbrook body. It was one of a pair of Leyland Leopards (WVH 230-1), which were numbered 101-2, before being taken over by Yorkshire Traction, when 101 became 389.* Strathwood Library

Bottom Right: *Venturing to the back of the County Motors garage, I was rewarded with this view of three Roe-Bodied double-deckers. Numbers 82 and 94 are Guy Arabs, while 88 is a Leyland Titan.* Robert Berry Collection.

Conclusion

This then, has been a personal glance back to a time when Huddersfield was not packed with cars, there was no 'ring road' a small number of traffic lights and no motorways. It is a time when Huddersfield was founded on its traditional industries, and its populace took pride in their work and pleasure in their hobbies. Watching cricket, athletics or rugby league at Fartown, or the First Division Huddersfield Town side at Leeds Road were vital parts of people's leisure time. More gentle pastimes could be noted in the beautiful grounds of Beaumont Park, Greenhead Park, Norman Park and Ravensknowle Park, or in the magnificent Town Hall listening to concerts such as those given by the Huddersfield Choral Society or the Brighouse & Rastrick Brass Band. It is also a time when many families aspired to saving up for their first small car, or even a motorcycle combination.

Above *Huddersfield Corporation Transport department did not survive quite long enough to celebrate its centenary, but as a concession WYPTE painted two buses in the former Huddersfield Tramways and JOC liveries. Of these, PUA 299W is seen ascending Woodhouse Hill.*
Robert Berry Collection

Yet for the majority, this was still a time when municipal or private bus companies were plentiful, well organised and operated by friendly and courteous staff. Between them they afforded a stress-free and civil method of commuting to work, going on day or evening excursions, or for getting away on a traditional family holiday. My special thanks to H. John Black, Tony Blackman, The Strathwood Library (who can be contacted via **www.strathwood.com**, for copy slides of their images that are used in this book) and all the many others who have assisted me in some way or another.